Fifty *More* Homilies from the Deacon's Desk

Deacon Rick Wagner

ISBN 979-8-89428-430-9 (paperback)
ISBN 979-8-89428-432-3 (digital)

Copyright © 2024 by Deacon Rick Wagner

All rights reserved. No part of this publication may be reproduced, distributed, or transmitted in any form or by any means, including photocopying, recording, or other electronic or mechanical methods without the prior written permission of the publisher. For permission requests, solicit the publisher via the address below.

Christian Faith Publishing
832 Park Avenue
Meadville, PA 16335
www.christianfaithpublishing.com

Printed in the United States of America

This book is dedicated to my beautiful wife, Carol. Through her battle with cancer, she has shown me and many others what it means to be a positive, faith-filled person. She makes me better by her example.

Acknowledgments

Thank you to my friends and coworkers Krista and Sheryl for proofreading my work and helping to transform it from the spoken word to the written word.

Thank you to my lifelong parish, St. Pius X Catholic Church in Indianapolis, and all its parishioners for your continued support and encouragement.

Cover artwork: *From the Pulpit*, courtesy of my wife, Carol.

Love Is a State of Being

Fourth Sunday of Ordinary Time   Jeremiah 1:4–19
                                        1 Corinthians 12:31–13:13
                                        Luke 4:21–30

Some people might be surprised to discover that I, like many of you, am an expert on love. I mean, I love *so* many things; I must be an expert.

Allow me to impress you with my lengthy love list.

As you know from a past homily, I love Billy Joel's music. I love Will Ferrell movies. I love sandwiches from Penn Station and cookies from Subway. I love Diet Coke. I love the fact that I can now order breakfast any time I want from McDonald's. I love smoked sausage. I love fishing early in the morning when the water is as smooth as glass. I love laying in the hammock with a good book. I love football.

Oh, and I love my wife…and my kids…and my grandkids.

My point in sharing this random list of the things I love is to illustrate how the word *love* has saturated our everyday vocabulary. Our understanding of the word has become convoluted.

Love can mean to enjoy something or to have a passion for it. Love can mean to have an attraction or to be drawn to something. It can be an action or a feeling. It can be a noun or a verb.

This ambiguity allows me to say, "I love my wife and I love smoked sausage" in the same sentence, which seems ludicrous—as I'm sure Carol would agree.

So when we hear today's second reading, it may be difficult to understand the love Paul is referring to in his letter to the Corinthians.

He defines love by telling us what love is: "Love is patient, love is kind."

He defines love by telling us what love *is not*: "Love is not jealous or rude or ill-tempered."

He emphasizes the power of love: "So faith, hope, love remain, these three; but the greatest of these is love."

Paul's words are beautiful. It is no wonder that couples so often include this scripture passage in their marriage ceremony.

However, because the English language has allowed the word *love* to morph into so many other realities, we might still struggle to understand the love Paul is describing to us. Seeking understanding, we ask ourselves, "What is our *experience* of the love he describes?"

Paul's letter was written in Greek. The Greek-speaking people also experienced many different types of love. However, they were smart about it. They used several unique words that allowed them to distinguish among the different types of love.

Eros was the word used to describe a passionate love. *Phileo* was used when the Greeks referred to a fondness or affinity for something or someone—perhaps even Diet Coke or smoked sausage. *Storge* was a word used to describe a natural affection for those who were closest to them.

The word Paul chose to use in the original text was *agape*. Agape is the Greek word used to describe a self-giving love, one that gives without demanding or expecting repayment. It is love so great that it can be given to even the unlovable or unworthy. It is love that continues to love even when it is rejected. It is the type of love God has for us; He is totally committed to our well-being without regard for our worthiness.

This selfless giving would explain why the word *agape* is sometimes translated as *charity* and might help us understand how *we* are called to love.

Jesus said, "Love God with all your heart…and love your neighbor as yourself." Love God and love others.

I can handle the "love God" part, but "love others" is tricky. If that means I have to love everyone I meet, I'm afraid I would fail. As hard as I try, there are days that I don't even *like* everyone I meet.

However, if we keep the word *charity* in mind, it seems possible. I'm not sure I could love everyone I meet, but I'm sure I could be charitable to them. It seems easier to *be* something than to *do* something.

One of the most powerful illustrations of the concept of love that I have ever heard did not come from St. Paul or from a personal understanding of the Greek language.

It came from a simple story about a young girl in the Philippines.

Ed and Eileen Johnstone are parishioners here at St. Pius. Eileen is a coworker of mine and shared the following story with me. It was reported by her son, Luke, and her daughter-in-law, Katie:

> Luke and Katie, married for just over a year, made a commitment last August to devote time to mission work. They are working in the Philippines and will be for the next two years. Luke does the purchasing for several local orphanages, and Katie works with the poorest children living in the slums of the city.
>
> They had been preparing for several weeks for the big Christmas Mass for the children. Nearly 1,500 children, the children they serve, would be there, with the archbishop of Manila celebrating the Mass.
>
> After the Mass, the archbishop gave any child wo was interested the opportunity to come forward, say their name and age, and share what they wanted to be when they grew up. As one can imagine, with 1,500 kids many were interested, so the line was quite long.
>
> The children in the line stated their name and age and then shared that they wanted to be doctors, nurses, teachers, and so on. Since it was the first year, Katie and Luke were at this Mass. They kept wondering when the archbishop

would say, "Okay, that's all for today." He never did; he just kept listening.

Finally, there was only one little girl left. This girl was from an orphanage for children with special needs. She had Down syndrome. She came forward and said her name and her age. Then the archbishop asked her what she wanted to be when she grew up.
She said, "I want to be *loved*."

That is the love about which St. Paul wrote. That is the love we are called to offer one another.
Love is not an action or a feeling. It is not a noun or a verb. Love is a state of being.
What a simple yet powerful message: Don't just love, *be* love.

January 2016

Control Enthusiast

Second Sunday of Lent   Genesis 15:5–18
                               Philippians 3:17–4:1
                               Luke 9:28–36

Perhaps you've seen the recent television commercial for National Car Rental. The customer wanted things done his way—the *right* way. He chooses National Car Rental so he can bypass the check-in counter, get into whatever car he wants, and drive away. He never has to engage in conversation with another human being. He has total control, which is the way he likes it.

The commercial begins with the man saying, "I've been called a control *freak*. I prefer to think of myself as a control *enthusiast*."

In 2010, *Psychology Today* offered an online quiz to help determine whether or not one might be considered a control freak. For the purposes of the quiz, a control freak was defined as a person who feels a need to prove himself, be in charge, or get his way.

Here is a sample of some of the questions from that quiz:

- Do you dislike depending on others, accepting help from them, or allowing them to do things for you?
- Do you "help" other people drive—tell them what route to take, when to turn, and where to park?
- Are you the one who steps in and orders people around?

I took the quiz, and it might surprise my wife to hear that based on my score, I am *not* a control freak. However, I did fall into the second category, which indicated that I do have some control issues that might need to be addressed.

I prefer to think of myself as a control enthusiast.

Two weeks ago, we heard the story of Peter dropping his nets and following Jesus. He gave up his livelihood and left his family behind to follow a nomadic preacher. While this is certainly impetuous, we are not alerted to any control issues he might have had at that point.

However, there are other examples from Peter's discipleship that tell a different story.

We saw it at the Last Supper when Peter initially refused to allow Jesus to wash his feet. Remember the control freak quiz?

Peter disliked depending on others or allowing them to do things for him.

How about the occasion when Jesus asked, "Who do you say I am?"

Peter answered with confidence, "You are the Messiah, the Son of the living God."

Jesus then shared that He was indeed the Christ and, because of that, must suffer greatly. Peter would have none of it! "God forbid, Lord!" he said. "No such thing shall ever happen to you."

He helped Jesus drive and told Him what route to take.

Today, we have another example. Peter was a witness to the transfiguration of Jesus. What a gift to be there as Christ was once again revealed to him! Without taking any time to process what he had seen, he immediately began planning.

Peter said to Jesus, "Master, it is good that we are here; let us make three tents, one for you, one for Moses, and one for Elijah."

He jumped right in—*He was the one who stepped in and ordered other people around.*

Peter was a control freak. Luke was quick to call him out in today's Gospel. He wrote, "But Peter did not know what he was saying." As a disciple, Peter often did not know what he was saying. He was so intent on maintaining or assuming control that he didn't take it all in. He didn't take the time to just listen.

So God was very deliberate in His words to Peter and the others: "This is my chosen Son; *listen* to him."

The word *listen* is found in scripture over four hundred times. It must be important.

How many times has God invited *us* to listen? How many times do we actually do it? What keeps us from hearing what He has to say?

Maybe you don't listen because you are unable to filter out the noise of the world. You are bombarded with sensory messages and are unable to decipher which messages are important and which are simply fleeting sound bites.

Perhaps your image of God is that of an aloof superpower that moves the chess pieces of humanity around on a giant board. You pray to Him when you need something, but why listen? You don't expect Him to actually answer you.

Or maybe you are that control enthusiast I've been talking about, the person who chooses not to listen to anyone else.

As Dr. Phil might ask, "How's that working out for you?"

Listening to others, even if it is God, means taking the focus off of us and our own needs. It means veering off the path we had planned and giving up at least partial control. It might mean having to learn to trust. None of this is easy for a control enthusiast.

However, listening is our access to understanding. We should accept God's invitation to listen. It is particularly important during the Lenten season when we are called to bring ourselves into right relationship with God.

Can you imagine trying to improve or rekindle a relationship with a friend or loved one without ever having a conversation with him?

Relationships are built on two-way communication. How can we have a personal relationship with God if we're doing all the talking? As you've heard me say before, prayer is not a monologue.

Listening is a critical component of the relationship. In order to be intentional in our listening, we must occasionally seek silence. "Be still and know that I am God."

The following was written by Sister Mary Clare, a Carmelite nun:

> God cannot be found in noise and agitation. In silence, God listens to us. In silence, listen to Him. In silence, God speaks to our souls, and the power of His word is enough to transform our very being. We cannot listen to God and to the world at the same time. We need the sacred space that silence creates in order to turn our undivided attention toward God even if it is only for a few precious moments of our day.

If you are one who likes control, use that to your advantage and take control of your time. Choose to spend some of it in silence. Choose to listen.

During this Lenten season, seek silence and listen to what God has to say to you.

Consider becoming a *listening* enthusiast.

February 2016

Mercy Has a Sound

Fifth Sunday of Lent   Isaiah 43:16–21
                            Philippians 3:8–14
                            John 8:1–11

If you have been in a baby products store lately, you have probably noticed that there are a number of sound machines available on the market. These are electronic devices that reproduce sounds that are comforting to babies, allowing them to fall asleep more easily. With the push of a button, parents can select sounds such as "Ocean," "Summer Night," "Rain Forest," or "Waterfall."

I can relate. For many years, I slept with an oscillating fan near the bed. I am not sure why, but I found the whirring of the small motor comforting. Comfort has a sound.

When our kids were going through their teenage years, Carol and I laid in bed feigning sleep until we knew all of them were home, safe and sound. Curfew was approaching, or perhaps curfew had come and gone, and our anxiety elevated. Then there was a sound—the sound of a key sliding into the lock on the front door, and relief washed over us. Relief has a sound.

My daughter Laura once shared with me that she liked the fact that she was short in stature because when she hugged me, her ear was right over my heart. She said my heartbeat seemed to be saying, "I love Laura…I love Laura…I love Laura." Despite some concerns that I might have an irregular heartbeat, I was pleased that Laura connected the sound of my heart to my love for her. Love has a sound.

In today's Gospel, we discover that *mercy* has a sound.

I used the following words from John to help me picture the woman who had been brought to Jesus: "Then the scribes and the Pharisees brought a woman who had been caught in adultery and made her stand in the middle."

Although John does not provide us with the details of the agony the woman was experiencing, this is what I saw in my mind as I read the Gospel story:

She was forced, pushed and shoved, into the middle of a circle of bloodthirsty men who were eager to stand in judgment. They relished the thought of delivering the punishment the woman was due. Can you even imagine the shame and humiliation she must have felt? Or the level of fear she was experiencing? The sheer gravity of what she had done and the fate awaiting her had to have been overwhelming.

Anticipating the wrath of those who condemned her, she dropped down to her knees. She leaned forward, with her head nearly touching the ground. She covered her head with her arms in what would have been a futile attempt to ward off the stones. Each second seemed like an eternity as she waited for the first stone to be thrown.

The woman *must* have been terrified. After all, we heard in the Gospel, "Now in the law, Moses *commanded* us to stone such women."

This was not up for debate. She was going to die. It was the law.

She waited as the outcry from the Pharisees continued. Then Jesus spoke, and it grew quiet. She braced herself for the certain onslaught of stones. However, it never came.

There was absolute silence. Then she heard it—the sound of a single stone hitting the ground. Then she heard another and another. Stone after stone hit the ground, not thrown but dropped. Mercy has a sound.

With the sound of each stone hitting the ground, she experienced a greater sense of self-worth. Shame was replaced with repentance.

She uncovered her head cautiously and rose up from the ground. Looking around, she saw the men who had brought her to Jesus walking away. She had not been condemned and punished. Instead, she was shown mercy. Through the power of Jesus, she was forgiven.

In the Gospel, we heard, "Then Jesus said, 'Neither do I condemn you. Go, and from now on do not sin any more.'"

She no longer felt afraid but reborn. Facing certain death, she was given new life. Not condemned by Jesus but loved. That is the power of mercy and forgiveness.

Are you the woman in the story? Are you ashamed of some of the things you have done, afraid to face God, and incur His wrath and punishment?

Or maybe you feel like you *deserve* to be punished. You deserve to have stones hurled at you and are unworthy of mercy and forgiveness.

Are you one of the Pharisees in the story? Do you stand in judgment of others, eager to point out their faults and add to their punishment? Do you refuse to offer compassion and forgiveness to one who has hurt you?

After all, what's right is right, and what's wrong is wrong. Rules are rules, and it's your job to make sure the guilty party suffers. If that is the case, perhaps you should look down at the ground and see what Jesus is writing in the dirt.

The adulteress woman was not the only person to hear the sound of mercy in today's Gospel. With the help of Jesus, each Pharisee was able to see his own sins in the sins of the condemned woman. He was able to hear the sound of his individual stone hitting the ground. That sound represented a "letting go" of judgment.

Whether we experience mercy or offer mercy, we are restored to new life. We leave the past in the past and move forward.

Our other readings today deliver that same Lenten message.

Today's first reading is from Isaiah: "Remember not the events of the past, the things of long ago consider not; see, I am doing something new!"

And from Paul's letter to the Philippians: "Forgetting what lies behind but straining forward to what lies ahead, I continue my pursuit."

Mercy has a sound. When you seek reconciliation or pray for forgiveness, close your eyes and listen carefully. You will hear the sound of the stones of condemnation hitting the ground one by one. Take in the sound and embrace the new life it offers.

You can also *deliver* the sound of mercy, opting not to cast the stone at those who have offended you but rather to drop it at your feet. Give others the opportunity to experience the new life offered by your mercy, and in so doing, be renewed yourself.

Mercy has a powerful impact on those shown mercy as well as on the merciful. "Blessed are the merciful, for they will be shown mercy."

March 2016

Barn Loft Faith

Fourth Sunday of Easter   Acts 13:43–52
Revelation 7:9–17
John 10:27–30

In our thirty-three years of marriage, Carol and I have discovered that when it comes to deciding how we spend our leisure time, we don't have all that much in common.

I like to go fishing. Carol doesn't even like to eat fish, much less catch them.

Carol likes to draw and paint. I have neither the talent nor the patience for either.

I could spend an entire day watching a *Seinfeld* marathon and laugh at every episode. Carol didn't think the show was funny when we watched it in the '90s.

Carol could sit on the beach for days. I get restless within minutes.

However, in recent years, Carol and I have discovered a hobby that we both enjoy and can do together. We like going to flea markets, thrift shops, and yard or barn sales. We both enjoy this activity but for different reasons. I like digging through piles of stuff to find the diamond in the rough. The deeper the piles are and the dirtier the stuff, the more enjoyable it is for me.

Once I've had my fun, I turn it over to Carol. She doesn't like the digging through dirty stuff so much, but once I have found a hidden treasure and presented it to her, her creativity kicks into high gear. Her thoughts turn to how she can restore this item that has lost its luster or give it new life by giving it a new purpose.

Occasionally, she will sell the repurposed item at a much lower price than it would cost at a store or in its original form. We usually take that money and go out looking for another hidden treasure. It's not about the money. For us, it's the idea of turning one man's trash into another man's treasure.

For example, in the loft of a barn, we might find two worn out dining room chairs that the owners believe have lost their usefulness. We buy them for $5 each. They are cleaned, refinished, or repainted; reinforced where weak; and given colorful new seat padding. Then they are fastened together; they are no longer two chairs but one bench.

The person who had given up on the chairs might have a new appreciation for them. The person who did not have a need for two chairs might be attracted to the newly created bench. For the person who could never have afforded a new bench, it is now within reach.

We like restoring the value of something—both the value of the item itself as well as the value it may now hold for a number of different people.

The first reading today from the Acts of the Apostles is about the repurposing of faith. The apostles told the Jews, "We brought the Word of God to you first, but you rejected it."

The Jews, entrenched in years of tradition and stubborn in their beliefs, stored their faith in their barn loft, and they were fine with that. Most of them rejected the repurposed faith the apostles were offering.

A few, referred to as Jewish Christians, had a new appreciation of their faith. They were grounded in the traditions of the Jewish faith—the two worn chairs—but accepted and appreciated the repurposed faith, the bench. They formed a small community of Jews who accepted Jesus as the Christ.

Rejected by so many in Jerusalem, the apostles announced, "But since you reject it, we now turn to the Gentiles." They traveled outward from Jerusalem, making themselves available to a broader audience.

The Gentiles had an appreciation for what Peter and Barnabas were bringing to them. They never expected to be included or to be invited into a faith community. Gentiles were considered pagans who did not know the true God. Many Jews took such pride in their own culture and religious heritage that they considered Gentiles unclean, calling them dogs.

The Gentiles were unchurched. They didn't even *own* chairs, and now they were being offered two newly restored chairs in the form of a bench. Scripture tells us, "The Gentiles were delighted when they heard this and glorified the word of the Lord." One man's trash was another man's treasure.

The apostles realized that their repurposed faith was not appreciated in Jerusalem and took it to the streets, making it accessible to the common man, to the masses. The second reading from the Book of Revelation also speaks to the idea of gaining a broader audience: "I, John, had a vision of a great multitude, which no one could count, from every nation, race, people, and tongue."

This strategy apparently worked. From its humble beginnings, there are nearly 2.3 billion Christians in the world today.

In his column in this week's edition of *The Criterion*, Archbishop Tobin discusses how we should view our faith:

> Christians shouldn't act like our faith is a burden or that Christian life is made up of an endless series of oppressive rules and regulations. We should be joyful—rejoicing in God's love for us.
>
> Easter joy should give us the confidence we need to overcome the negative voices that are around us all the time. It should help us smile, enjoy ourselves, and give thanks to God always.
>
> Christians can be joyful because God has reached out to us and loved us. We are not alone; we are God's people who gather into the Church and are united in Christ. Our faith should bring us lasting joy.

Does your faith bring you lasting joy? Perhaps the totality of your faith was routinely going to Mass on Sundays.

After a time, it transitioned to *usually* going to Sunday Mass, then *sometimes* going, and finally, going to Mass twice each year.

How can something we do so seldom bring us joy?

Or perhaps you continue to go to Mass every Sunday, but it is nothing more than a ritual. You are simply going through the motions.

How can something you do with no passion bring you joy?

If your faith is worn out and gathering cobwebs in the barn loft, it is time to bring it back to life. Dust it off and appreciate it as you did when it was new. Stabilize it where it has grown weak. If your faith is only defined by attendance at Sunday Mass, make it into a bench and add something to it to make it more meaningful and useful: Try going to daily Mass occasionally, add the Liturgy of the Hours to your day, pray the Rosary, read Scripture, join a Bible study, volunteer, serve others. *Live* your faith!

How could a life built on faith *not* bring you joy?

Many of you know that a young teacher at Bishop Chatard, Kyle Guyton, died suddenly and tragically about ten days ago. Just a few days after his death, in a memorial service we held in a packed gymnasium, this is what Kyle's Mom had to say: "God has a plan, a purpose for this. Who knows what it is? I surely don't. But I'm thankful. I'm thankful and blessed and have joy in my heart to have been used as a vessel to be Kyle's mom."

This came from a single parent who had lost her only child. She is a witness to all of us. She is living a life built on faith and experiencing lasting joy even in the darkest of times.

Is it time to repurpose your barn loft faith?

Make an effort to restore its value. Allow it to bring you lasting joy!

April 2016

Being Christian Defined

Solemnity of the Ascension of the Lord Acts 1:1–11
Ephesians 1:17–23
Luke 24:46–53

We are nearing the end of the Easter season, celebrating the Ascension of the Lord today and looking toward Pentecost next week.

Through the readings of the Easter season, Jesus has been preparing us, saying, "I will be leaving you soon, but I will send you the gift of the Holy Spirit."

Today, it happens. He ascends into heaven and leaves us to carry on His work, the work of discipleship. What does it mean to be a disciple? What beliefs and actions define us as Christians?

All three readings today point us toward the answer and help us define what it means to be a Christian:

From the Acts of the Apostles: "You will receive power when the Holy Spirit comes upon you, and you will be my witnesses." To be a Christian is to be a witness of Jesus Christ to others.

From Paul's letter to the Ephesians: "May God give you a Spirit of wisdom and revelation resulting in knowledge of him." To be a Christian is to truly know God.

From John's gospel: "Thus it is written that the Christ would suffer and rise from the dead on the third day and that repentance would be preached in his name to all the nations." To be a Christian is to preach in His name.

I have two images to share with you that help further define what it means to be Christian (projected onto the front wall of the church).

The first image is a recently created icon in memory of the twenty-one Coptic Christians killed by ISIS in February 2015. The Coptic Church is the largest Christian Church in Egypt. Twenty-one members of the church were working as migrant farmers in Libya when they were captured by ISIS and brutally killed on the beaches of the Mediterranean Sea.

ISIS went one by one, asking each Christian, "Are you a follower of Jesus Christ?"

If he answered, "Yes," he was killed.

It was discovered later that one of the migrant workers who was captured by ISIS, pictured in the middle of the icon, was *not* a Christian. He *was* an Egyptian migrant worker but not a member of the Coptic Christian Church.

When ISIS approached him and asked if he was a follower of Jesus Christ, he could have said no and would have been telling the truth. He could have saved his own life by revealing that he was not a Christian.

However, he watched the others die courageously and saw how strong their faith was. He saw them, one by one, answer with a confident "Yes!" when asked if they followed Jesus Christ.

When ISIS asked this man, this non-Christian, if he was a follower of Jesus Christ, he responded, "I want their God to be my God." He said this and was killed.

The faith in Jesus Christ shown by the others was so strong that someone who witnessed it was willing to die.

This made me think: What if a non-Christian followed me around every day? What if he watched how I lived *my* life—how I interacted with others or how I treated those less fortunate? What if he watched what I did when no one else was around?

Would watching me make a difference in his life?" Would he say, "I want his God to be my God?"

I share the second image in honor of Mother's Day.

In the picture are Devrone and his mother, Merlene, who live in a small village in the West Indies. A birth defect has caused his feet to remain underdeveloped, so he cannot walk.

There are no roads from their village to the nearest town. There is only a narrow, rocky path. Since her son was six years old, Marlene has carried him to school every day. He is now twenty-one years old and a junior in college. He will graduate from college next year.

This mother has carried her son to school every day for fifteen years. She has loved him completely. She has loved him sacrificially. She has loved him with a mother's love.

What if a non-Christian followed *Marlene* around every day? Would seeing how she lived her life make a difference in his life? Would he say, "I want her God to be my God?" or "I want to love like she loves?"

I challenge you to stand in front of the mirror before you go to bed tonight. Ask yourself one or more of the Christian-defining questions you've heard this morning:

- Am I a witness of Jesus Christ to others?
- Do I truly know God?
- Do I preach in the name of Jesus?
- When people watch how I live my life, do they say, "I want his God or her God to be my God"?
- Do I love with a mother's love?

If you answer no to these questions, do not be discouraged. You are in good company. Remember the apostles and how they were huddled in hiding behind locked doors?

They, too, were unsure of how to carry on the work of Jesus, unsure of how to live the life of a Christian.

Help is on the way. Pentecost comes next week. Like the apostles, if we are open to the gift of the Holy Spirit, we will be given the courage to come out from behind locked doors and proclaim the good news to all the nations.

May 2016

Make Your Life a Living "Amen!"

Solemnity of the Most Holy Body and Blood of Jesus Christ

Genesis 14:18–20

1 Corinthians 11:23–26

Luke 9:11–17

Today is the Feast of the Body and Blood of Jesus Christ. We use white altar cloths and wear our celebratory vestments.

We remember the passion and death of Jesus at every Mass, but today, we celebrate in a special way the gift He gave us—the gift of Himself, the gift of His Body and Blood. It is the Real Presence of Christ in the sacrament of the Eucharist.

On this feast day, we focus on the beauty of this gift and on the ways we show our gratitude. After all, the word *Eucharist* means *thanksgiving*.

Each time we receive the gift of the Body and Blood, we give thanks by saying "Amen." Amen—"I believe." We are stating publicly our belief in the Real Presence of Christ in the Eucharist.

You may be wondering why the gospel reading chosen for today's feast was that of the feeding of the five thousand. The well-known story of the multiplication of the loaves and fishes is certainly an impactful gospel, but why not focus on the Last Supper? Why wouldn't the Church choose the story of the *Institution* of the Eucharist to mark this feast?

As we heard in the second reading, Paul made *reference* to the Last Supper. In his letter to the Corinthians, he recounted the words Jesus used: "This is my body. This is my blood. Do this in remembrance of me."

However, for the *gospel* reading, the Church asks us to reflect upon the miracle story of Jesus feeding the five thousand. Why? What messages does the Church hope to pass along on this feast day?

There are many. I will share two.

First message: When we turn to Jesus with conviction in our hearts, He responds with abundance.

The five thousand were not just given enough to get by. *They all ate and were satisfied. And when the leftover fragments were picked up, they filled twelve wicker baskets.* He responded to the needs of the people with abundance.

With His Body and Blood, He feeds us and sustains us. He provides us with everything we need. In fact, He provides us with things we may not even know we need. Jesus did more for the five thousand than satisfy their hunger. He fed them spiritually as well.

Pope Francis tells us, "Jesus gives himself to us in the Eucharist, offering himself as spiritual food that sustains our life."

Where are we turning when we need to be fed? Are we turning to Jesus or to worldly things?

Drugs and alcohol, sex and pornography, materialism—so many things of this world that are calling out to us, offering to meet our needs, to fill the void in our lives. However, this food does not sustain us, and whatever satisfaction we experience from it is fleeting at best. We are not left with a feeling of gratitude but of shame.

When *Jesus* feeds us, all will eat and be satisfied. He responds with abundance.

If we *are* turning to Jesus, is it with conviction in our hearts? Do we truly believe He can and will help us? Or are we just going through the motions? Go to Him with confidence. When you say "Amen!" let the words come straight from your heart.

Second message: Gift-giving with Jesus is not a one-way street. We are called to give a gift in return. Saying "Amen" shows gratitude, but it does not end there. He gave of Himself for us. We must give of ourselves for Him.

We see this demonstrated for us in the first reading. We heard that the high priest Melchizedek "brought out bread and wine" for

Abram to feed him and restore him to full strength. We are told Abram responded to this gift by offering the priest a tenth of everything he owned.

We also hear this message subtly in the gospel. The disciples recognized the needs of the five thousand hungry people, and their first thought was to send them away. Jesus told them, "Give them some food yourselves."

He knew the disciples could not produce the necessary food to feed the people. However, by saying, "Give them some food yourselves," He was planting a seed with them. He wanted them to see how He responded to the needs of those who turned to Him.

When the people came to him, He responded with abundance. He wanted the disciples, and wants us, to witness His generosity. He wants us to respond to the needs of others in the same way. Whether it is hungry stomachs or hungry hearts, we are called to feed others.

When I hand a sandwich to a homeless man, I am feeding him physically. However, he is fed in other ways. The very fact that I am there shows him that someone cares. When I speak with him, he experiences human interaction and compassion. It's more than a sandwich.

When people ask me to pray for them or for one of their loved ones, I do it. I will often stop what I'm doing and offer that prayer right away. Or I will make a note to myself so I won't forget. That person is fed by the prayer but also by knowing that I made their request a priority. And because my prayer joins with theirs, it becomes communal prayer and in communal prayer there is power. It's more than words.

When one student chooses to sit next to another student who eats his lunch alone day after day, that formerly isolated student is fed. Someone noticed him. Add conversation to it, even a little, and doors are opened. He has value. He is not alone. It's more than a chair in a cafeteria.

Share the gifts you have received. Like Jesus, respond to the needs of others with abundance.

Appreciate the gifts Jesus offers you:

- His Body and Blood offered to you at every Mass
- His abundant response to your needs when you turn to Him

In return, show Him your gratitude.
Saying "Amen" is not enough.
Make your life a *living* "Amen!"

May 2016

A Few Minutes in My Favorite Chair

Thirteenth Sunday in Ordinary Time   1 Kings 19:16–21
Galatians 5:13–18
Luke 9:51–62

I purchased two identical plaques from the gift shop at Saint Meinrad. One hangs on my office wall at school, placed in such a way that I see it each time I exit the office. The other is hanging in our family room, visible to me as I sit in my favorite chair.

The plaques read simply, "Remember What's Important."

I need to see that message regularly. At school, it offers me a gentle reminder that no matter how busy we are, we cannot lose sight of what is most important—serving the young people entrusted to us. I need to see it at home as well, reminding me to think outside of myself.

Perhaps you can relate to the following scenario: This occurred in the month of May several years ago. Things had been crazy at work. We were engaged in wrapping up the current school year, as well as hiring teachers and planning events for the following year. It was a busy day at school, followed by a late afternoon meeting. Afterward, I stayed around for some athletic events being held on campus. The workday ended with an evening meeting.

I arrived home at around 9:30 p.m., exhausted. Carol was already in bed. I had nothing on my mind other than collapsing in my favorite chair. I didn't want to think about or do anything.

Just as I sat down, I received a phone call from my daughter, then a senior in college. She asked if I could look at the email she sent me earlier and read over the draft of the resume she had been working on. Sure, I can do that. I read through it and offered my advice.

While I had my email open, I noticed I had a message from my son, who was finishing up his freshmen year in college. Normally, I would have closed my laptop and read that email the following day. However, it was marked URGENT. Nothing was ever urgent in Robby's world, so I was intrigued.

He had received word from the financial aid office that one of the forms we had completed needed additional documentation. The deadline to submit was the next day. It should be noted that the message from the financial aid office was three weeks old. What made it urgent was that Robby waited until the night before to let me know about it. An hour later, that was finally done.

As I finished up my dad duties, Carol walked into the room. She had heard me come home earlier and thought I might have fallen asleep in my chair. She said she hadn't been able to sleep because of an issue she was struggling with at work. So I switched to husband mode and focused some attention on Carol, listening to the details of her day, offering whatever comfort and advice I could.

It was nearly midnight by that time, and as I eased out of my chair, the plaque caught my eye: "Remember What's Important." Seeing that message, I realized I had not yet taken time for my evening prayer. Carol joined me in prayer before we retired for the day.

I am not so self-absorbed to think that my busy life is any busier than anyone else's. *Life* is busy—the inbox of our lives is overflowing.

Our response cannot be to simply collapse in our favorite chair. If we do, we risk losing sight of what is most important.

If you were paying attention to our readings today, you heard two nearly identical stories. In the reading from 1 Kings, Elijah had been instructed by God to anoint Elisha as his successor.

We heard it told in this way: "Elijah went over to him and threw his cloak over him. Elisha left the oxen, ran after Elijah, and said, 'Please, let me kiss my father and mother goodbye, and I will follow you.'"

In the gospel, word had spread about Jesus, and He had people interested in becoming His disciples. Luke told it like this: "And to another Jesus said, 'Follow me.' But he replied, 'I will follow you, Lord, but first let me say farewell to my family at home.'"

Two very similar situations. Someone was called by God, and the immediate response was to make an excuse. In both stories, we heard, "Yes, but something else is a priority right now." In other words, let me sit in my favorite chair for a while and think about it.

Where the stories differ is in the follow through—what was the ultimate response of those who were called?

If we go beyond today's reading in the Gospel of Luke, we learn that many potential disciples opted *not* to follow Jesus. His teachings were too difficult. He asked too much of them. They were focused on their own needs and lost sight of what was most important.

However, with Elisha, it was a different outcome. He was simply going about his work when Elijah threw a cloak over him and told him he was to be the next great prophet called by God. It would not have been unreasonable for Elisha to say, "No, thank you" to this sudden turn of events.

However, Elisha understood that God does not choose us the same way we choose one another. God sees our hearts and knows what we are capable of far better than we know it ourselves.

We are not told whether or not he went home to kiss his parents goodbye or not, but we do know his next move as detailed in the first reading: "Elisha took the yoke of oxen and slaughtered them. He burned the plowing equipment for fuel to boil their flesh, and gave it to his people to eat. Then Elisha left and followed Elijah."

Elisha was literally burning bridges behind him. He was going to do God's will, and there was to be no turning back. The destruction of the plowing equipment would have made it impossible for him to return to his former manner of living. His prompt response signified a radical change. His decision to follow Elijah, to answer God's call, was both immediate and permanent.

Without mentioning Elisha by name, Jesus certainly seemed to be referring to him when He said, "No one who sets a hand to the plow and looks to what was left behind is fit for the kingdom of God."

What a perfect message for this ordination weekend. Six men in the Archdiocese of Indianapolis were ordained to the priesthood yesterday and now serve as examples of the radical change that is a part of answering God's call.

In order to follow Jesus, we have to stop thinking worldly thoughts. We must plow forward and never look back. We have to think and act as Jesus and keep our eye on the ultimate prize of heaven.

God calls all of us, not just once in a lifetime, but day after day. Are we prepared to hear the call and answer it?

Quoting the plaque, we must "Remember What's Important."

Nothing is more important than God's will for you…not even a few minutes in your favorite chair.

June 2016

There Are No Feeding Frenzies in Heaven

Eighteenth Sunday in Ordinary Time   Ecclesiastes 1:2, 2:21–23
Colossians 3:1–5, 9–11
Luke 12:13–21

    I want to share a fascinating thing I have discovered about the homeless population: When offered food, blankets, or other basic necessities, they do not take more than they need. It would certainly be justified if they did. Why not grab a second sandwich? Who knows when they will get another chance to eat?

    I noticed this phenomenon in my very first encounter with homeless people on a trip to San Diego years ago.

    Carol and I walked from our hotel through downtown San Diego one morning to attend Mass at a nearby church. There were homeless people *everywhere*—sleeping on every park bench, in the doorway of every place of business, leaning up against every trash can or dumpster, in the alleys, in the little park in the center of downtown—*everywhere*. We saw literally hundreds of homeless on our ten-block walk to the church. This was a completely new experience for us.

    After Mass, we stayed in church for a short time, praying about what our response should be. We felt like we had to do something. On our walk back to the hotel, we stopped at a bakery. We gathered what money we had and bought as much as we could from the bakery display case.

We assumed it wouldn't last long—assumed the first few homeless people we encountered would grab whatever they could. I guess we were picturing a piranha feeding frenzy of some sort.

That is not what we experienced at all. The first person we approached took one item and thanked us. We extended the bag toward him and asked if that was all he needed. His response: "There are lots of folks out here. You go help them."

The next person kindly declined the offer of food: "I had a good meal last night. I know some of these people haven't eaten for days." Then he pointed to a family nearby and said, "I know they need food."

We went to the family. It was a husband, wife, son, and baby daughter. The husband was so gracious and appreciative. He took a bagel and handed it to his son. He took another and tore it in half, giving half to his wife and hungrily biting into the other half himself. He waved me off when I held the bag in front of him to take more, thanking me again.

It went on and on like that. No feeding frenzy. No squirreling away more for later.

I have worked with the homeless population in Indianapolis for nearly six years now. My experience over those six years has been the same. The homeless take only what they need at the time. Not a week's worth, but only enough to make it through another night.

I couldn't help but think of my homeless friends as I read today's gospel.

Gospel writers often included descriptors that allow us to get a sense of a person's motive or intent when he or she approached Jesus. They identified the person as a Pharisee, a widow, a Gentile, a tax collector, and so on.

However, on occasion, the evangelists wrote generically about nameless people who were present at the time. They wrote, "A *man* approached Jesus" or "a *crowd* gathered around Jesus."

I like it when that happens. Those nameless people often hold the key that unlocks the message that God has embedded in scripture.

And while I can't relate to being a Pharisee or a tax collector, I *can* relate to being an everyday man or part of a crowd. So when the gospel writer gives me the opening, I climb inside the gospel and become that unnamed person. I want to live that experience.

The gospel passage I read moments ago began with the words "*Someone* in the crowd said to Jesus, 'Teacher, tell my brother to share the inheritance with me.'"

If I'm that guy—that "someone in the crowd"—what was I doing? What in the world was I talking about?

Jesus was not known as a mediator, so I was not *really* asking Him to help negotiate with my brother over an inheritance, was I?

What I think I was doing was looking for an outlet for my frustration. I was trying to mask my frustration, but Jesus didn't bite. He dismissed my phony request by saying, "Friend, who appointed me as your judge and arbitrator?"

He read between the lines. He understood my frustration and knew even before I did what I really wanted to say.

What I wanted to say was, "It's just not fair! Why do other people have more stuff, better stuff? Why does God choose favorites? Why are there haves and have-nots? More importantly, why am I one of the have-nots?"

Maybe you find yourself asking those same types of questions. Not out loud, of course; we hide our frustration like I did in the gospel. If we do complain out loud, it is behind closed doors with others who share our frustration. Misery loves company so together we gossip. We jealously criticize those around us who have more money, own bigger houses or newer cars, and take exotic vacations.

As that "someone in the crowd," I wanted Jesus to affirm me. I wanted Him to tell me I was right. Then after affirming me, I wanted Him to fix it. I wanted Him to arrange for me to get a bigger piece of the pie.

However, Jesus didn't bite on that either. Instead, He saw my request as a teaching moment. He told a parable that offered a "get over yourself" message. He told of a man who was preoccupied with acquiring wealth, building a bigger barn in order to warehouse his surplus grain and store away more than he could possibly ever use.

The parable ends with God telling the man that he had wasted his time. He was going to die that night and all that grain would do him no good.

God's message to the man was similar to the familiar phrase: "You can't take it with you."

This focus on self, this desire to acquire things to satisfy one's own desires, is the vanity to which the first reading refers.

Vanity is the single-minded focus on self. However, vanity is also the frustration I felt as the "someone in the crowd." I may not have been focused on acquiring things, but I was obsessed with what others had. It was me-centered thought.

Obsession and jealousy are examples of vanity too: "All his days sorrow and grief are his occupation; even at night his mind is not at rest. This also is vanity."

You only have so many hours in a day. If the majority of your time is spent on acquiring temporal things or obsessing over what others have, how much time do have you left for God?

Tell me how a man spends his time, and I'll tell you what he values.

The familiar saying is, "You can't take it with you." However, when it comes to heaven, perhaps we should say, "You don't need to take it with you."

You'll have everything you need; there are no feeding frenzies in heaven.

July 2016

Embrace the Mystery

Twenty-second Sunday in Ordinary Time   Sirach 3:17–29
Hebrews 12:18–24
Luke 14:7–14

There are some themes in scripture that are repeated over and over again. Scripture is God's Word, so the repetition of these themes is God's way of saying, "Pay attention! This is important!"

One of those themes is humility.

In today's first reading from Sirach, we heard, "My child, conduct your affairs with humility. Humble yourself…and you will find favor with God." And in the gospel, "For every one who exalts himself will be humbled, but the one who humbles himself will be exalted."

One way to think of humility is in terms of knowledge and control. When we are not being humble—or "exalting ourselves" as the gospel says—we claim knowledge and understanding of all and, thus, feel in control. Being humble means recognizing that we do not have all the answers and are willing to give up control, willing to trust.

Human beings love being in control. Not understanding something, or being unable to explain it, makes us uncomfortable.

I am certainly not "anti-knowledge." We should strive to understand and explain the world around us. The problem comes when we encounter things we cannot explain.

Take for example, our faith. Faith, by definition, is trusting in something we cannot explicitly prove. There are so many unknowns, so many mysteries when it comes to our faith and when it comes to God.

Doubt is inherent in our faith. Faith challenges us. The way many people handle that challenge is to reject what they don't understand. Maybe you are one of those people.

If so, I invite you to embrace the mystery. If you don't understand, seek to know more. In the meantime, embrace the mystery.

For example, I can't explain God. I can't show you a picture and say, "This is God, and here is proof of His existence." I can't explain God, but I know when I've experienced Him. And I can share my experience of God with others. Some things are meant to be experienced, not explained.

Recently, I had a very vivid dream. Carol, Carol's sister Maureen, and I were being chased. I do not know by whom or why.

We ran into a huge building. It was apparently a warehouse for water bottles and sports drinks. There were pallets of Gatorade everywhere.

We made our way through the warehouse and exited the building on the opposite end. Once outside, Carol and I realized Maureen was no longer with us. We turned back toward the building, and in a panic, Carol called out, "Maureen! Maureen! Maureen!"

Just then I woke up. The reason I woke up, I discovered, was because Carol, sound asleep next to me, was calling out, "Maureen! Maureen! Maureen!"

Isn't that fascinating?!

After thirty-three years of marriage, we even dream together! How cool is that?

I have shared that story with some people, and they immediately went into explanation mode: "Well, the reason that happened is probably because you were in REM sleep. You subconsciously heard Carol calling Maureen, so you incorporated that into your dream."

Stop! I don't need an explanation! I don't even want an explanation. I have the experience. Just let me be fascinated.

Let me ponder the possibility that my life with Carol is so intertwined, and we are so much in love that the two of us have truly become one.

Our oldest daughter, Mary, is due with her second child any day now. I remember when she had her first child, our first grandchild, six years ago. Carol was already in South Bend. I was not able to make it there until a few hours after the birth of little Joseph.

When I walked into that hospital room and saw Mary holding him, my head was spinning, and my knees almost buckled. It was surreal. There in front of me was my baby…holding a baby. What a gift! The circle of life on display right before my eyes. There was almost a glow radiating from the bed. I felt a whole range of emotions—joy, wonder, awe.

I remember saying aloud, "My baby is holding her baby…how did this happen?"

Of course, my son, always a smart aleck, answered, "Do you need me to explain it to you, Dad?"

Despite my rhetorical question, I didn't need an explanation or even want an explanation. I just wanted to take in the awe and the wonder. I just wanted to embrace the mystery and experience the moment.

I return now to the topic of faith and God, mystery and experience.

When the Bishop Chatard students were in the horrific accident in June, I joined hands with nearly 150 people in the surgery waiting room and prayed with them.

I can't explain God, but I *experienced* God in that prayer and in that moment. I *felt* God in our midst, and I know others did as well.

When I was ordained a deacon, I knelt before Bishop Coyne. He laid his hands on my head and prayed these words: "Lord, send forth upon him the Holy Spirit that he may be strengthened by the gift." With those words, I felt the gift of the Holy Spirit. Afterward, I was unable to accurately describe that feeling to my family. I could not find the words. I couldn't *explain* it, but I definitely experienced it.

Isn't that what faith is—no explanation, just experience? Trusting in something we cannot explicitly prove?

Accept the challenge of your faith. Risk feeling uncomfortable and not in control. "Humble yourself…and you will find favor with God."

Don't reject what you don't understand; you will miss out on the experience.

Embrace the mystery!

August 2016

There Are No Do-Overs

Twenty-Sixth Sunday of Ordinary Time   Amos 6:1–7
1 Timothy 6:11–16
Luke 16:19–31

When we were growing up, a bunch of us used to get together to play whatever sport was in season. We played in a vacant lot next door to my friend Greg's house.

The lot was almost perfect. It was level ground and big enough to fit a good-sized football field or baseball diamond. It was lined on one side with trees, so we had a place to park our bikes and get a few minutes of shade as needed.

There was only one small problem. There were power lines that ran overhead, hanging slightly lower than they should have been.

This was not often an issue. However, once in a while, a long pass in a football game or a well-hit ball in a baseball game would hit one of the wires and drop to the ground.

After much debate, the decision was made that if the ball hit one of the wires, it was an automatic "do-over." We just wiped the slate clean—that play or that pitch never happened. A second chance.

In fifth grade, I had Sister Scholastica for Math class. She was a good teacher, but most of us were scared of her. She was strict and a little on the mean side.

There was one thing we *did* like about Sister Scholastica. If most of the class didn't do well on a test, she gave the entire class a do-over. She actually called it a "dummy do-over," which didn't help with her reputation for being mean.

On those occasions, she passed back our papers and told us how disappointed she was with us. She reviewed all the math problems, explained them, and pointed out where we went wrong. Then she put a wastebasket in front of the room and dramatically announced the need for a "dummy do-over." One by one, we went to the front of the room, tore our test in half, and threw it in the trash.

The next day, we took the test again. We got a do-over; our first attempt never happened. We were given a second chance.

Who doesn't appreciate getting a do-over?

That being said, today's readings remind us that we are given one life to live on this earth. Unlike childhood ball games and math classes, there are no do-overs!

All three readings speak to the dangers of complacency. They create a sense of urgency. We have one opportunity to do the work God asks of us, one opportunity to show our gratitude to Him. When I speak of doing God's work and showing our gratitude, I present them as one and the same.

What is His work? We hear the answer loud and clear throughout the New Testament: *Love God. Love others. Serve God by serving others.*

When we do this work, we are at the same time showing our gratitude for the life we've been given.

At a recent funeral I attended, I heard the following words that capture this sentiment well: "Every breath you take is a gift from God. Everything you do should be an expression of gratitude."

In today's readings, we are called to action. Do it now! Don't put it off! You never know when your time on this earth will come to an end.

In his letter to Timothy, Paul tells us we must live a life pleasing to God to show our gratitude: "But you, man of God, pursue righteousness, devotion, faith, love, patience, and gentleness. Compete well for the faith."

Pursue and *compete* are not passive words. They are words that call us to action. When we wake up each day, we must focus on living a life of love and service. We make a deliberate decision to be a man or woman of God.

We *pursue* such a life. Pursue implies that we cannot stand still. Such a life will not come to us. Rather, we must "get after it." There is a sense of urgency, a call to action.

"Compete well for the faith." Compete implies that there is an opponent. Our opponent is in the very world in which we live. We may wake up *intending* to pursue "righteousness, devotion, faith, love, patience, and gentleness" just as St. Paul suggests.

However, we walk out into a world that preaches an entirely different message. A world that lacks faith and even rejects God. A world promoting love of self. A world not of patience and gentleness but of intolerance and violence.

So if our plan is to be a man or woman of God and to pursue a life that glorifies Him, we will have a fight on our hands. This pursuit is countercultural, so we will need to *compete* if we are to be successful. If we put off the fight to another day, if we are complacent, we lose.

As the prophet Amos said, "Woe to the complacent!" Amos offered a clear warning, a call to action.

We see the result of complacency in Luke's gospel. We heard the story of the rich man who was unprepared when his time on this earth came to an end. The gospel tells us, "The rich man also died and was buried" *and found himself in* "the netherworld, where he was in torment."

The man had all the material wealth he could ever need while on earth. That is what he pursued and competed for each day. As he sat in his "purple garments and fine linens and dined sumptuously," I'm sure he was quite satisfied with his achievements.

He likely gave *himself* credit for his material success. Rather than thank *God* for all the gifts he had been given, the rich man grew complacent. He failed to express his gratitude despite having the opportunity to do so each day.

Lazarus was a poor, sick, homeless man living right on his doorstep. The rich man's "pursuit" was only a few steps away. Yet he never offered Lazarus a meal, not even leftover scraps. He never offered him clothing or shelter. He stepped over Lazarus each day as he ventured from his palatial home, proud that he had made such a great life for himself and embarrassed for this pathetic man.

On second thought, maybe I am being too rough on the rich man. Maybe he *intended* to help Lazarus. Perhaps he was thinking, "When I *get a chance*, I'll invite Lazarus into my home, perhaps even give him some of my old clothing I don't need anymore. *Someday*, I'll bring him a meal. Maybe *tomorrow* I'll chase the dogs away, clean his sores, and spend some time with him."

Well, when he *gets a chance* never happened. *Someday* never came. *Tomorrow* never came. His life on earth ended. His opportunity to show his gratitude died *with* him.

You have been called to action. The way you live your life each day matters. We only have this one life; there *are* no do-overs.

September 2016

Zacchaeus versus the Grinch

Thirty-first Sunday of Ordinary Time   Wisdom 11:22–12:2
2 Thessalonians 1:11–2:2
Luke 19:1–10

I might be the only one who recognized this connection, but as I read the familiar gospel story of Zacchaeus, the image of another popular character kept popping into my head. Zacchaeus seems to have quite a bit in common with the Grinch of Dr. Seuss fame. (I said I might be the only one…)

For example, Zacchaeus was the chief tax collector. He was also the chief sinner, and the townspeople wanted nothing to do with him.

It was said of the Grinch, "You're a mean one, Mr. Grinch. I wouldn't touch you with a thirty-nine-and-a-half-foot pole."

Zacchaeus extorted the people, stealing their money.

The Grinch stole all the Christmas presents and decorations, including the candy cane of little Cindy Lou Who.

Zacchaeus experienced conversion, coming down quickly and receiving Jesus with joy.

The Grinch experienced conversion, and it is said that his heart grew three sizes that day.

We'll come back to conversion and the changing of hearts later.

Luke wrote in his gospel: "Zacchaeus was seeking to see who Jesus was; but he could not see him because of the crowd, for he was short in stature. So he ran ahead and climbed a sycamore tree in order to see Jesus, who was about to pass that way."

It would appear that his sole motivation was a desire to see Jesus. However, I believe there was more to it.

I'm sure you have seen this safety decal on many trucks. It says, "Warning: If you can't see my mirrors, I can't see you."

Yes, Zacchaeus needed to see Jesus, but he also needed *Jesus* to see *him*.

The question is, *why?*

Why did Zacchaeus need to see Jesus? And *why did he need Jesus to see* him*?*

Here is my theory on the first question. Jesus had made quite a name for Himself as He traveled from town to town, teaching and preaching. He built up a substantial number of followers. He was unlike other prophets. Scripture tells us that people noticed Jesus "spoke with authority."

In other words, He didn't tell people of God's hope for the world. He told them specifically what needed to happen, how they needed to live their lives. He made many uncomfortable with such talk, yet they were still drawn to Him.

Jesus was captivating. He spoke of *people* being more important than *things* and *love* being more important than *success*. His definition of riches centered on the kingdom of heaven, not on what people accumulated here on earth.

Jesus's reputation and message preceded Him. Zacchaeus was, by earthly standards, an extremely rich, successful, and powerful man. Yet he was moved by this new message. The words of Jesus touched his heart.

He began to question his priorities. He felt guilt and remorse. Reflecting on his life was suddenly a painful endeavor. He had doubts about everything he knew as real in his life. While it was disconcerting, there were seeds of joy planted as well. There was a hint of excitement about the possibilities that lie ahead. Zacchaeus had never felt that way before, and he didn't understand it.

When he heard Jesus was coming through Jericho, he didn't just *want* to see Him; he *needed* to see him. Words were just words; he needed to see the man who spoke those words in order to make them come to life. He didn't care what it looked like for the chief tax collector of the town to run to the sycamore tree and begin to climb.

He *needed* to see Jesus.

The second question is, *why did Zacchaeus need Jesus to see him?*

To know *of* Jesus, or to see Him from a distance, was not enough. What was stirring in Zacchaeus was the desire for a *relationship* with Him. He needed Jesus to really know him, to look into his heart and see the real Zacchaeus—not the powerful chief tax collector but rather the lonely man who was hurting inside.

He needed to reprioritize his life and eliminate the pangs of guilt and the pain he was feeling. He wanted to explore those seeds of joy and that sense of excitement he felt.

He needed to be loved and forgiven, and that happened for him almost immediately.

Upon seeing Zacchaeus, Jesus said to him, "'Come down quickly, for today I must stay at your house.' And he came down quickly and received him with joy."

Zacchaeus's heart grew three sizes that day. He received Jesus with joy because it was clear that *Jesus* wanted a relationship too.

Years of pain poured out. He told Jesus, "Behold, half of my possessions, Lord, I shall give to the poor, and if I have extorted anything from anyone, I shall repay it four times over."

Because Jesus touched his heart, Zacchaeus took the next step. He sought out Jesus, laid his sins at His feet, and resolved to live a better life in the future.

In return, Jesus offered forgiveness, saying, "Today salvation has come to this house… For the Son of Man has come to seek and to save what was lost."

Compassion and mercy—the Sacrament of Reconciliation revealed. Conversion takes place.

What is keeping you from seeking Jesus? What is keeping you from climbing up that tree for the opportunity to see and be seen? What is keeping you from building a relationship with Him?

Is it your focus on accumulating earthly wealth? You spend all your time and effort on your job so that you can make more money and acquire more things, so there is no time left for Jesus?

Is it fear that keeps you from seeking Jesus? Seeing Jesus and having Him as part of your everyday life will mean acknowledging that you are no longer in control. *His will be done* is an unsettling option.

Is it shame? Your sinful life has piled layer upon layer of guilt and shame on you. You don't see Jesus because you don't *want* to see Jesus. And you certainly don't want Jesus to see *you*. He could not possibly love someone as unlovable as you, right?

Allow Jesus to touch your heart. Like Zacchaeus, receive Him with joy. In return, you will be shown compassion and mercy.

Who knows, maybe *your* heart will grow three sizes that day.

October 2016

Knack for Being Wrong

Third Sunday of Advent

Isaiah 35:1–10
James 5:7–10
Matthew 11:2–11

I'm sure my wife would agree with this statement: I am often wrong. I don't want to go so far as to say I'm an expert at it, but I do think I'm well above average. Something like that doesn't happen overnight; it's perfected over time.

I have embraced my knack for being wrong. I own it.

Here is one example of many: I was a freshman in high school. Our first algebra test was coming up. The day before, Mrs. McCurdy spent the entire class period reviewing for the test. I dozed off for part of the period. I drew some pictures in the margins of my textbook. I finished up some English homework. I flirted with the cute blonde who would eventually become my wife.

Mrs. McCurdy also offered a practice session prior to school the next morning. Several of my friends went but not me. Math always came easy to me. I didn't need to pay attention to the review or attend any practice sessions.

I was wrong. I failed the test.

I assumed my mom would understand. I had never failed a test before, so I felt certain she would cut me some slack.

I was wrong. She was quite upset with me.

Despite her anger, I knew she would keep it between the two of us. No need to bother Dad about this.

I was wrong. And Dad was quite upset too.

Certainly, grounding me was not an option. How was grounding me going to make me better at math? That made no sense.

I was wrong. I was grounded for a week.

My first high school dance was the following weekend. I knew I was grounded, but my parents weren't heartless. I was positive that they would lift the grounding and allow me to go.

I was wrong. I was not allowed to go the dance. I was allowed, however, to work on algebra all night.

You get the idea. And again, this is just one example of many.

It came to mind as I began working on this week's homily. As I read today's readings in preparation, I made an assumption that turned out to be wrong.

During Advent, we look forward with joyful anticipation to the coming of Jesus on Christmas day. Our first reading from Isaiah and the gospel from Matthew share what the experience of His arrival will be like.

From Isaiah, we heard, "Then will the eyes of the blind be opened, the ears of the deaf be cleared; then will the lame leap like a stag, then the tongue of the mute will sing."

Much the same, we heard in the gospel, "The blind regain their sight, the lame walk, the deaf hear."

I could imagine the pure joy of receiving these remarkable gifts; I could imagine the rejoicing that must have taken place. Someone once blind, who had lived his life in darkness, could now see! Someone deaf, never able to hear leaves rustling in the breeze or to hear someone say her name, could now hear! Someone who was lame could not only walk but could *leap like a stag*! Someone mute suddenly had a voice. Such beautiful, awesome gifts!

I am happy for the blind and the deaf and all who benefit from these gifts. But what does that have to do with me? After all, I am not blind or deaf or mute or lame.

In looking over some commentaries on today's readings, I came across one that read, "If you believe these readings are not intended for you…if you believe you are not blind or deaf or mute, you're wrong."

I'm used to being wrong, but these words made me reflect on *how* I was wrong. This is what I realized about myself:

I pass by people every day in need. I get so focused on myself that nothing else comes into my field of vision. Others are reaching out to me, but I don't see them…I mean, *truly* see them. I must be blind.

The noise of the world is all around me. Others need me, and I am quite capable of helping them. There are people crying out for help, but I don't hear them…I mean, *truly* hear them. I must be deaf.

As a Christian, I am called to be the voice for the voiceless. I am called to speak on behalf of those who cannot speak for themselves—the unborn, the elderly, the homeless, and the disenfranchised. God is listening; He is waiting for me to speak for them—*truly* speak for them—but I say nothing. I must be mute.

There are so many ways that I could be actively engaged in serving others and, in so doing, serve God. I convince myself that someone else will take care of the needs of others. The world is in need of servants—true servants—but I take no steps to help. I must be lame.

I *am* blind and deaf. I *am* mute and lame. I thought these readings were only for other people. *I was wrong.*

The bad news is I have a lot of work to do.

The good news is I am in the midst of the Advent season and have time to prepare, time to begin that work. If I am diligent in my efforts, I will be transformed. Along with others who are blind or lame, I will be able to rejoice at His coming.

In the second reading, in the letter from James, we are given our preparation instructions: "Make your hearts firm, because the coming of the Lord is at hand."

What does it mean to "make our hearts firm"?

We have often heard the scripture passage from Psalm 95: "If today you hear his voice, harden not your hearts."

So God wants us to have *firm* hearts but not *hardened* hearts. What is the distinction?

A hardened heart is closed off to the needs of others. It beats only to sustain itself. A firm heart has resolve. It fights through indifference and beats for the community as a whole. It beats to God's rhythm. A hardened heart is indifferent. A firm heart is merciful, attentive, and charitable.

Pope Francis described a firm heart as "a heart that allows itself to be pierced by the Spirit so as to bring hope to our brothers and sisters."

If you think these readings aren't intended for you, *you're wrong*. If you think you have no work to do, or don't need to prepare, *you're wrong*. If you think you're not at least partially blind or deaf or mute or lame, *you're wrong*.

However, you can combat these limitations by making your heart firm and opening yourself to the gift of Jesus. And there's *nothing* wrong with that.

December 2016

I've Never Been Punched in the Nose

Third Sunday in Ordinary Time   Isaiah 8:23–9:3
1 Corinthians 1:10–17
Matthew 4:12–23

We read these words at the beginning of the Gospel of John: "In the beginning was the Word, and the Word was with God, and the Word *was* God."

God is alive in scripture. Through scripture He speaks to us—to give us hope, to provide comfort, or to instruct us.

The beauty of scripture is that it speaks to us individually. We have a personal relationship with God, so His messages to us are personal. Each person receives the message he or she is intended to hear.

However, I propose there are times when scripture holds a universal message for all believers. Certain scripture passages are intended to shake us up or call us to task; they are "wake-up calls" for the Church.

Today, we heard such a message. In no uncertain terms, God tells us, "Do the work I have called you to do or the life, death, and resurrection of My Son were all in vain."

It is a challenging message and may make us uncomfortable; and that, too, was God's intent.

Listen again to these words from the prophet Isaiah: "The people who walk in darkness have seen a great light; on those who dwell in a land of gloom, a light shines. You have brought them abundant joy."

There are many in our world who "walk in darkness" or "dwell in a land of gloom." It is *light* that they need—it is *light* that will destroy the darkness and *light* that will bring hope to the land of gloom.

Here is the challenging, and possibly uncomfortable, reality: *We* are the light. *We* are responsible for bringing them abundant joy. You, me, believers everywhere—it is *our* responsibility.

Before heading off to find your flashlights, listen again to what Paul had to say in his letter to the Corinthians: "For Christ did not send me to baptize but to preach the gospel…so that the cross of Christ is not emptied of its meaning."

We are the great light, and we radiate that light when we preach the gospel. We must do it, or the cross has no meaning. The suffering Jesus endured was in vain.

The fact that this directive makes us uncomfortable is not surprising. What an incredible responsibility. However, it is what we signed up for when we became intentional disciples and what we are called to do as apostles.

We don't need to go to Monument Circle and shout scripture into a megaphone in order to "preach the gospel."

We simply need to *share* our faith with our words and *reveal* our faith by our actions.

So what are we afraid of?

I gave a retreat talk last year to a group of senior students. When I was speaking with a student afterward, she said, "I wish I could do what you just did."

When I asked her what she meant, she said, "You talk so easily about God and your faith. I wish I could do that."

I asked her why she couldn't do that. Her response was one I've heard many times: "I guess I'm afraid. I don't want people to think I'm a religious freak."

I encouraged her to talk about what excites her and let people think what they will.

This young lady is not alone. Many people share her fear. They feel that publicly expressing their beliefs or sharing their faith will cause them to be negatively judged by others.

I find it fascinating. When people talk about their jobs, sports, or fashion, I don't negatively judge them as career freaks or sports or fashion freaks. Why is faith different?

There is a radio show called *Busted Halo*. The host of the show, Fr. Dave Dwyer, was asked the question "What can I do to get over the fear of talking about my faith in public?"

In his response, Fr. Dwyer offered two points to consider:

- First, the fear of what will happen if we share our faith is much worse than what *actually* happens.
- Second, the positive possibilities of sharing our faith far outweigh whatever it is we are afraid of.

I understand what Fr. Dwyer was saying. Here are some personal examples:

I have led many staff meetings over the last ten years. I have conducted hundreds of interviews with teacher candidates. I have also had my share of difficult meetings with parents.

In each of these situations, I have begun the meeting with prayer. Never once has anyone stormed out of the room or attacked me for sharing my faith. As a matter of fact, people have often thanked me for beginning our time together in that way.

When our food arrives at a restaurant, Carol and I join hands across the table and offer a premeal prayer. Never once has the waitress taken the food back, and no one at the surrounding tables has ever gotten up to leave in disgust. Quite the opposite—we have had people tell us how refreshing it is to see people praying in public.

While waiting in a long checkout line at Walmart, I overheard the couple behind me talking about Catholics in a less-than-flattering way. I shared with them that I was Catholic and asked them if I could answer any questions for them. The man seemed bothered that I said anything and ignored me. However, the woman said she had a question regarding our "obsession with Mary."

I shared some of our beliefs about Mary, and she seemed to appreciate the information. I couldn't help but notice the older woman in front of me was listening too.

I don't know if I changed the hearts of the young couple that day, but I do know that I didn't get punched in the nose, and I was not verbally assaulted.

Once outside of Walmart, the older woman was waiting for me. She thanked me for talking to the couple inside. She said she was Catholic, too, and I had given her the courage to speak up if she is ever in a similar situation.

Which brings me back to my conversation with the senior girl on retreat. I suppose she was right—speaking about her faith may cause some to label her a religious freak.

However, that is a small price to pay.

If sharing your faith brings light to just one person "walking in darkness," it is worth it.

If it brings hope to just one person living in a "land of gloom," it is worth it.

If it brings "abundant joy" to just one person, it is worth it.

If it gives just one person the courage to do the same, it is worth it.

What would happen if you stood up at the next big meeting and said, "Would anyone mind if I begin with prayer?"

What would happen if you said to a coworker during your break, "I was really moved by the scripture readings I heard at Mass on Sunday."

Or to a friend, "I am going to say a special prayer each morning during prolife week, would you like to join me?"

Talk about what excites you, and let people think what they will.

Don't allow the cross of Christ to be "emptied of its meaning." Don't allow the suffering and death of Jesus to be in vain.

January 2017

Inviting Others to the Dance

Sixth Sunday of Ordinary Time   Sirach 15:15–20
                                     1 Corinthians 2:6–10
                                     Matthew 5:17–37

I have a sad story to share.

When our son was in high school, the school staff conspired against him. They intentionally went out of their way to keep our son in the dark. For instance, the school hosted major events for the kids, such as dances and bonfires and movie nights, and told *everyone* in the school *except* Robby.

Here is one specific example: Robby was a sophomore in high school. It was a Saturday night. Carol had read in the last few school newsletters that there was to be a dance that night, so she asked Robby why he wasn't going. He knew nothing about it. The fact that there was a dance that night was completely foreign to him.

Thinking she had misread the information, Carol double-checked herself. Yes, the newsletter confirmed there was a dance that night. Robby's response, "Well, they didn't tell us about it."

We were fascinated by this, so we asked, "You're saying there is a dance at your school tonight, and the students weren't told about it?"

"Nope."

Carol challenged him: "I've talked to a few of the parents. I know some of your *friends* are going to the dance. Someone must have told them."

Then came Robby's familiar response: "Well, no one told *me*."

An interesting side note: Over four hundred kids attended the dance.

One of our friends was a teacher at the school, and we shared the dance story with her. She laughed. She told us there were handwritten signs broadcasting news of the dance about every five feet throughout the entire building. She said it was publicized on the daily announcements each morning and tickets to the dance were sold every day during lunch periods for nearly a month.

I may be going out on a limb here, but I am going to guess that some of you have a child similar to our son. The child whose backpack you have to clean out on a regular basis to gather up the crumbled permission slips and health forms. The child who often seems oblivious. The child who needs a one-on-one personal invitation to engage with what is going on around him.

Hold on to that thought.

Very seldom in scripture do we see a reference to free will—man's ability to make choices. In today's first reading from Sirach, we heard: "He has set before you fire and water...to whichever you choose, stretch forth your hand. Before man are life and death, good and evil, whichever he chooses shall be given him."

God gave man the gift of free will. However, free will is a double-edged sword. On the one hand, we are blessed with the ability to make our own choices.

On the other hand, the following are some paths that lead us to the *wrong* choice:

- Perhaps we make our decisions based on what society *tells us* is acceptable.
- Maybe we simply respond to our own immediate needs and desires.
- Or we fail to take into account *God's* will for us.

There is a piece that often gets lost when considering the God-given gift of free will. That is, we have a responsibility to make *informed* decisions.

We must inform our *minds*. We do this by

- using prior experiences to inform future behaviors—learning from our past,
- doing our due diligence—thinking through the impact of the decisions we face,
- or drawing on the wisdom and expertise of others we trust to *help us* make informed decisions.

We must also inform our *hearts*. We need to spend time in prayer and reflection in order to discern *God's* will for us.

What do you believe God's plan is for you? Do you think you are using your God-given gifts as He intended? How can you incorporate God's will for you into your decision-making?

You may be sitting in the pew, wondering, "What does this homily have to do with me? I don't have a child like Deacon Rick describes, and I am quite capable of making informed decisions on my own."

You may be right, and if you were a disciple *only*, watching out for yourself might be enough. However, we are part of an apostolic Church. As apostles, we have a responsibility to teach, lead, and guide others. We are called to help inform the minds and hearts of those around us.

We must be a voice of faith and reason in a society spinning out of control. We must model selflessness. We must bear witness to God's presence in our lives by sharing our experiences with others. We must pray that God's will be done and encourage others to do the same.

Even doing all that is not enough. If you want your child to learn to cross a street safely, would you simply show him pictures of a street? Or read him a news story about a pedestrian being struck by a car?

No, you would take your child by the hand, stand at the side of the road with him, teach him to look both ways, and then walk *with* him. You love him and care for him, so it requires personal contact.

In so doing, you increase the likelihood that he will make good decisions when crossing the road in the future.

We must remember that there are some who do not pay attention to the handwritten signs or listen to the daily announcements. They need personal contact from someone who cares about them. They need to be *invited*.

Apostleship calls us to inform the minds and hearts of others. It may need to get personal.

Sometimes we need to invite others to the dance.

January 2017

It's Not about the Apple

First Sunday of Lent   Genesis 2:7–9, 3:1–7
                            Romans 5:12–19
                            Matthew 4:1–11

I did a lot of dumb things when I was a kid. Today, I will share just one example.

When I was a freshman in high school, I participated in track and field in the throwing events—shot put and discus. For those who may not know what a shot put is, it is a twelve-pound steel ball that is thrown for distance.

I would often bring a shot put home the day before a track meet so I could get in some extra practice. After practicing on one such occasion, my dad stopped me as I walked toward the stairs with my shot put. I explained to him that I wanted to put it with my uniform because I was afraid I would forget it. He explained *to me* that bringing a twelve-pound steel ball upstairs was an accident waiting to happen, and he instructed me to leave it in the garage.

I did as I was told, and sure enough, I forgot it the next morning. This did not make my track coach very happy.

So the *next* time I brought my shot put home, I quickly and quietly brought it upstairs and put it with my uniform. The next morning, I concealed the shot put in my sweatshirt and headed for the stairs. As I took the first step onto the stairs, I stepped on one of the sleeves of my sweatshirt, causing the sweatshirt, and the shot put, to be pulled from my hands.

I learned several things that day.

I learned physics. I learned that the force of a twelve-pound steel ball bouncing down a flight of stairs was sufficient to propel that steel ball completely through the drywall and the insulation and actually loosen some of the bricks on the exterior of the house.

I learned how loud my mom could scream. I don't imagine there could be a louder scream than the one coming from a mother who believes her son is falling down the stairs.

Finally, I learned finance. Did you know that in 1975 it cost $87 to hire a professional to repair a five-inch hole in drywall and re-mortar three exterior bricks? I know because I had to pay the bill.

In this situation, I gave into temptation and sinned. Dad made it very clear what the expectations were, but when tempted with something more expedient, something more desirable, I chose my own path. My sin was not the act of taking my shot put upstairs to my room. My sin was one of arrogance. My sin was thinking I knew better.

Such was the case for Adam and Eve in the Garden of Eden. The sin was not eating the apple; the sin was the arrogance it took to even approach the tree. Despite God making His expectations very clear, they were arrogant enough to think they knew better.

It is the root cause of our sinfulness. We fall victim to our own arrogance.

We *know* right from wrong. We *know* what God expects of us. However, when tempted with something we want to do but know is wrong, we play the arrogant "free will" card: "*I* can choose. No one can tell *me* what to do."

We are like children. Have you ever tried helping a young child do something for the first time—like tie a shoe or button a button on a shirt? He will pull away and say, "I can *do it* myself," although he clearly cannot.

We show the immaturity of our faith when we give in to temptation. Sin is rarely defined by a specific behavior. It is most often defined by an "I can do it myself" arrogance. When we say, "I can do it myself," we are telling God we know better.

This attitude is what caused Adam and Eve to approach the tree in the first place.

It is the type of attitude that puts us in harm's way. It is how "harmless flirting" with a coworker turns into much more. It is how "just checking out a website" becomes a pornography addiction. It is how "a little white lie" makes lying on a regular basis so much easier.

This is why we pray the Act of Contrition. We resolve "to sin no more, and to avoid whatever *leads us* to sin." It is not about the apple; it is about never approaching the tree in the first place.

Pope Francis recently spoke to a gathering of priests in Rome, and his words offer us hope. He said, "One thing is clear: Temptation is always present in our lives. Moreover, without temptation, you cannot progress in faith."

In other words, what doesn't kill us makes us stronger. It is okay to fall victim to our own arrogance, as long as we learn from it and grow stronger because of it. As we progress in our faith, our relationship with God is strengthened, and we become more resistant to temptation.

In today's Gospel, Jesus offered us the ultimate example of fighting through temptation. Three times, the devil offered objects of desire to Jesus—food, power, and worldly possessions. His humanity made Him vulnerable to temptation just like any of us.

When Jesus was tempted to turn the stones into bread, He did not say, "Maybe I'll turn *one* stone into bread and see how it tastes."

Jesus was told that all He had to do is prostrate Himself and worship the devil, and He would be given all the kingdoms of the world. Jesus did not respond with "Maybe I'll worship the devil *one* time just to see what it's like to have so many worldly possessions."

He avoided what would lead Him to sin. He never took a bite of the apple because He never approached the tree.

He could have given in to temptation. He could have said, "I know better than My Father," but He did not.

Instead, He chose the path that conformed to the will of God.

As followers of Jesus Christ, we make a commitment to do God's will. Temptation is inevitable. We will constantly be offered things the world tells us are better or easier or more desirable. However, we cannot allow arrogance to distract us from God's will.

The Lenten season calls us to get back on the right track. It calls us to prayerfully acknowledge the fact that we *do not* know better than God. It calls us to Reconciliation—"to sin no more, and to avoid whatever *leads us* to sin."

We won't put a hole in the wall if we never take the shot put upstairs.

We won't take a bite of the apple if we never approach the tree.

March 2017

At Least Leave the Door Open

Fourth Sunday of Lent

1 Samuel 16:1–13
Ephesians 5:8–14
John 9:1–41

At first glance, today's gospel reading offers a familiar two-part theme: The healing power of Jesus and the misguided tunnel vision of the Pharisees. Jesus gave sight to a man who had been blind from birth, and the Pharisees called Jesus sinful for performing this miracle on the Sabbath. While it is a familiar story and message, it is one that bears repeating.

However, in preparing the homily for this weekend, I felt like I should dig deeper; there must be something more. First, this gospel was chosen specifically for the Lenten season. There has to be a reason for such placement. Second, the story comes from the Gospel of John, and John's message is not always obvious. His gospel has layers that need to be peeled back.

So I read the gospel over and over. I compared this miracle of healing to those found in other gospels. Two differences emerged, both occurring at the very beginning of today's gospel passage.

Listen again: "As Jesus passed by he saw a man blind from birth. He spat on the ground and made clay with the saliva, and smeared the clay on his eyes, and said to him, 'Go wash in the Pool of Siloam.' So he went and washed, and came back able to see."

This point is interesting: The blind man did not ask to be healed, and no one else sought healing on his behalf. Think of the other stories of healing we've heard in the past: the blind or the lame calling out to Jesus, a paralyzed man on a mat being lowered down to Jesus through the roof, a centurion seeking healing for his son—"I am not worthy to have you come under my roof, just say the word and my boy will be healed," and a woman hemorrhaging for years reaching out to touch Jesus's cloak. People used whatever means necessary to be healed by Jesus.

That was not the case in today's gospel. "As Jesus passed by, he saw a man blind from birth." The blind man didn't call out. He did not seek healing. Why?

You may say, "Well, he was blind. He didn't know Jesus was there."

Jesus was well into his public ministry at that point. Everyone knew when Jesus was around. He traveled with an entourage—not only his disciples, but many others—the curious, those who had heard stories about him, some hoping to see a miracle, and some hoping to "catch him" doing something against Mosaic Law. Word spread quickly when Jesus was coming to town. It was very unlikely that the blind man would not know Jesus was there.

So why didn't he call out or send someone to ask Jesus for help?

Perhaps he did not consider himself worthy of being healed. He was blind from birth, and the prevailing thought of the time was that he deserved to be blind. He accepted his brokenness and his unworthiness. He was ashamed to reach out to Jesus for fear of rejection. He was afraid his unworthiness would be confirmed. In his own mind, he was too far gone.

Or maybe he lacked faith. He did not believe Jesus was capable of giving him his sight. Why call out when he didn't believe?

I noticed another difference between this healing story and others we find in scripture. It was a very elaborate healing. We know Jesus healed others simply with words or by touch or, in some cases, by being touched. Why the seemingly overcomplicated procedures of this healing?

I would like to offer two possible explanations. First, we learn that Jesus approaches each of us in a different way. Some he heals with a word, others with a touch. Some are healed remotely, and others face-to-face. Some seek Jesus; others are sought out by him. We are given evidence of the very unique and personal encounter each person, each of us, has with Jesus Christ.

A second aspect of the elaborate healing is its public nature. Jesus performed many miracles in private. He even made it a point at times to say, "Tell no one what you have seen." The healing in today's gospel was public by design.

Again, remember the entourage I mentioned—there were many people around when Jesus approached the blind man. The spitting on the ground, the mixing of dirt and saliva, the smearing of the paste on the man's eyes—a very unusual process that drew even more attention. But wait, we're not done...

The blind man was then sent to another location to wash. He would have needed an escort, and I am sure many people went with him out of curiosity. So picture this swarm of people, walking from that location, to the pool, and back again.

Then so many were amazed by what they saw that they took the man to the Pharisees. The swarm moved again and likely grew in size. The Pharisees very publicly rejected the explanation of the formerly blind man and threw him out and the swarm right along with him.

When Jesus and the man met again, John tells us the man said, "I do believe, Lord," and he worshiped Jesus as the growing swarm looked on.

Jesus was on his way to Jerusalem and ultimately to his passion and death. He was revealing himself more often. He used opportunities such as this to reveal the saving power of God. On that day, healing the blind man publicly offered an opportunity for God to be glorified. It was an opportunity to show what was possible, and that nothing was impossible with God.

So what is our Lenten message?

What is keeping us from seeking Jesus? We know he is around. We celebrate Mass with his entourage each week. We can see and feel the swarm.

Do you consider yourself unworthy? Do you feel like you do not deserve to experience his love and forgiveness? Are you ashamed of the baggage you carry with you? Are you afraid you will be rejected or have your unworthiness confirmed?

Or maybe you just lack faith. You have doubts about what Jesus is capable of, so why bother calling out to him?

The Lenten season is about working toward right relationship with God. If you are unwilling or unable to go to Him, at least leave the door open so he can come to you.

God's healing power is real. Nothing is impossible. Allow God to be glorified through you.

March 2017

Do You Only See God in the Rearview Mirror?

Third Sunday of Easter

Acts 2:14, 22–33
1 Peter 1:17–21
Luke 24:13–35

When my fellow candidates and I were in formation to become deacons, we might occasionally slip up and use the word *training* when describing the process of becoming a deacon. We would quickly be corrected by our director, "You are in *formation*, not in training."

The explanation was that when you train for something, you are preparing for a task. When you are formed, it becomes a part of who you are. We were not training to do the work of a deacon; we were being formed as deacons.

The formation process changed who I was.

I could point to several areas of transformation. However, as it pertains to today's gospel, I will share just one: The formation process helped me to recognize the presence of God in my everyday life.

This recognition was critical to my formation as a deacon. It is critical in the ongoing faith formation of all of us.

Perhaps you can relate to this experience: Prior to beginning my deacon formation, I only saw God in the rearview mirror. I was able to look *back* on periods of my life or look *back* on a specific event and see God's hand in it. However, like the disciples on the road to Emmaus, my eyes were "*prevented from recognizing him*" when He was right in front of me.

Formation has allowed me to experience and appreciate God in the here and now. There is great comfort in that.

A couple of examples come to mind. My granddaughter, Ellie, recently turned four years old, and it brought to mind the day she was born.

My memories are not only of the joy experienced with the birth of a healthy baby girl but also of the quiet just a few hours later.

It was raining outside. The hospital room was dark except for a nightlight. My daughter Laura and her husband had fallen asleep. Carol was holding Ellie, and both of them were asleep too.

In this snapshot of time, all was right with the world. I was at peace.

If I had been in that same hospital room prior to my formation, I would have described the scene as rainy, dark, quiet, and boring. However, my formation helped me to see it for what it was. It was time with God—Jesus sat in that hospital room with me.

In my joy, Jesus was there.

Following my dad's death three years ago, we sat in a funeral home in Chicago for his wake. My dad was a Marine, so at the end of the evening, a group of veterans processed in. One by one, they stepped in front of my dad's casket and solemnly and reverently saluted him.

I hadn't cried up to that point, but that scene got to me. As I tried to hide the fact that I was crying, I felt a small hand on my shoulder and turned to see my four-year-old grandson, Joseph. He just kept his hand there and smiled at me.

A few minutes later, my son-in-law took Joseph up to the casket to pay his respects. Joseph stepped in front of the casket and saluted my dad.

Prior to formation, that would have been just a cute grandson story. Because of my formation, I was able to see Jesus saluting my dad in the person of Joseph.

In my sorrow, Jesus was there.

There was no need to wait until later to experience those God moments in my rearview mirror. I was able to experience them in the here and now.

Today's gospel is a formation story.

The disciples on the road to Emmaus were walking away. They saw Jesus, the one they believed was the Christ, crucified right before their eyes. They watched Him die, and their faith died with Him.

Doubt, fear, and abandonment are all part of the faith formation process. In facing these challenges, our faith grows stronger.

The goal is not to be trained to use our faith as armor that we put on and take off as needed. The goal is to be formed in such a way that our faith is part of who we are.

This formation is possible when we believe Jesus is with us, and we allow Him to walk with us.

On the road that day, Jesus met the disciples where they were on their journey, ultimately revealing Himself to them. He literally turned them around. Suffering and death did not have the last word.

The burning in their hearts was their faith being reignited. It is what caused them to *"set out at once"* and return to Jerusalem with the good news—"The Lord has truly been raised!"

We have all been on a similar journey at one time or another. We are the disciples on the road to Emmaus. One minute our faith is solid; the next minute, we find ourselves walking in the opposite direction.

I believe there is much to learn from Cleopas and his companion. Despite the fact that their eyes were prevented from recognizing Jesus, their actions that day made an encounter with the risen Lord possible.

The two disciples welcomed a stranger and invited Him in—not once, but twice.

When Jesus approached them and interrupted their discussion, they could have ignored Him or told Him it was a private conversation. They did not. They were open to Him, engaged Him, and were attentive to what He had to say.

As they neared the end of their travels, Luke informs us that Jesus "gave the impression that he was going on farther." Jesus does not force Himself on anyone. The disciples could have cut ties with Him right then. But they didn't; once again, they invited Him in.

Jesus wants to have a personal encounter with us. He walks along with us on our road to Emmaus. He wants to be welcomed by us and to engage with us. He wants to turn us around and point us back to Jerusalem.

Are we allowing for that?

Or have we been hurt once too often? Has something happened in our life that has caused us to turn away from our faith? Is the pain preventing our eyes from recognizing Jesus when He is right in front of us?

If Cleopas and his companion had stayed entrenched in their sorrow and distress, they would have died a lonely and unfulfilled death in Emmaus. Fortunately, they did not. Even as they journeyed away from their faith, they remained open to the possibility of an encounter with God.

I pray that you remain open to that possibility as well.

Jesus wants to reignite our faith; He wants our hearts to burn. He awaits our invitation.

April 2017

Love Is an Action

Sixth Sunday of Easter

Acts 8:5–17
1 Peter 3:15–18
John 14:15–21

Carol and I celebrate our thirty-fourth wedding anniversary today. We work with quite a few engaged couples, and they often ask, "What's the secret to a successful marriage?"

I imagine what they expect to hear is a top-ten list that includes things like date nights, notes under pillows, breakfast in bed, foot massages, and surprise gifts. These are all wonderful things, and I'm sure Carol would be in favor of receiving all of them on a regular basis. However, when asked "What's the secret to a successful marriage?" my response does not include the items on that list.

My answer is simple: "Love your spouse."

The answer is simple. The day-to-day reality is challenging.

With my call to the vocation of marriage came the obligation to love Carol. That means waking up each day and making the commitment to love her that day. It is a part of my morning prayer.

How is that challenging?

We may have had a disagreement the night before. I might not even *like* her much that day, but I still need to commit to loving her.

Her annoying habits may be particularly annoying on a given day, but I committed to loving her, and her annoying habits are part of the deal.

I may be dealing with the stresses of a busy life and trying my best to keep all the balls I'm juggling in the air, but I still need to commit daily to making her a priority.

Each day Carol commits to loving me, and I *know* that is challenging. She is dealing with my annoying habits and her stressful life too and loving me in spite of them.

Love is not an emotion. Love is a decision. Love is an action.

The answer is simple: "Love your spouse." Doing the required work is challenging.

While you may appreciate this tutorial on marriage, you may also be wondering what this has to do with today's readings.

I believe we tend to overcomplicate the Word of God. Doing the required work of God is challenging enough; we should do our best to keep the message simple.

We are currently six weeks into the Easter season. We have been hearing messages of joy and hope in the resurrection.

However, as we head into these final two weeks of the Easter season, we will gradually notice a new message beginning to evolve. In today's scripture readings and in those we will hear over the next few weeks, there is a simple, yet definitive, call to action.

For instance, next Sunday, the Church celebrates the Ascension of the Lord. Jesus was taken up into heaven as stunned disciples looked on. Two men in white garments suddenly appeared and said, "Why are you looking up at the sky?" In other words, "Don't just stand there—get busy!"

The following Sunday, we will celebrate Pentecost. The disciples received the gift of the Holy Spirit. Their doors were unlocked, their fear was gone, and they went out to spread the Good News—again a "get busy" theme.

There are people who are hungry for the Word of God, who need to have their faith strengthened and affirmed. The creed we will profess in a few minutes makes our responsibility clear. We say, "I believe in one, holy, catholic, and apostolic Church."

One Church—the message of Jesus Christ is for everyone. The word *catholic* in the creed is not the capital "C" Catholic, meaning us here today—it is the lower case "c," which means *universal*. The message of Jesus Christ is not limited to those inside the walls of this building.

We are an apostolic Church. This fact is not merely because it was founded by and built upon the work of the original twelve but also because the word *apostle* means "one who is sent." An apostolic church is one whose members are sent out to spread the gospel message.

If we truly believe in *one, holy, catholic, and apostolic Church*, we accept the obligation to carry the Word of God out to the world.

The message is simple; doing the work is challenging.

The groundwork for this call to action is set with today's readings. We get a glimpse into three different strategies for carrying out this challenging work.

In the first reading, Philip takes a head-on approach when doing the work of the Church in Samaria. It should be noted how heroic this was. The Samaritans were not of pure Jewish blood and were considered "unclean" and to be avoided. However, in Samaria, as is the case in much of the world today, people were hungry for the Word of God. They took it all in.

In the first reading we heard, "With one accord, the crowds paid attention to what was said when they heard it…and there was great joy in that city."

Philip had so much success with his direct evangelization that he had to call for backup. It calls to mind the line from the movie *Field of Dreams*: "If you build it, they will come."

Some among you may be like Philip—bold and heroic, willing to stand in the middle of the courtyard and proclaim the Good News to whoever will listen.

Many of us are not like Philip but may be able to do as Peter suggested in his letter. In the second reading, he wrote, "Always be ready to give an explanation to anyone who asks you for a reason for your hope, but do it with gentleness and reverence."

We may lack the boldness of Philip, but if we study our faith and wear it on our sleeve, it may stir something in others who are hungry and searching. Seeing the confidence we have in our faith may lead them to ask us questions. Those questions then give us the opportunity to share our beliefs and explain the cause for our joy and our hope.

The third strategy for doing God's work comes directly from Jesus. In John's gospel, Jesus said, "If you love me, you will keep my commandments. And whoever loves me will be loved by my Father."

Which brings us full circle back to my marriage advice.

What is the secret to a successful marriage? *Love your spouse.*

What is the secret to a successful faith life? *Love God.*

That means waking up each day and making the commitment to love God that day.

The answer is simple. Doing the required work, regardless of the strategy you choose, is challenging.

Love is not an emotion. Love is a decision. Love is an action.

May 2017

Am I a Pretender?

Solemnity of the Body and Blood of Christ   Deuteronomy 8:2–16
1 Corinthians 10:16–17
John 6:51–58

Let me begin with a heartfelt Father's Day story:

A few years back, I was scheduled to give a talk at a parish and was sitting at our dining room table working on it. My son, Robby, came up behind me; put his hand on my shoulder; and asked what I was working on.

When I told him a had a presentation I was preparing for, he asked, "What's the topic?"

I told him, "It's a talk on effective parenting."

Any one of my other three children would have said something kind and encouraging such as "That's great!" or "You'd be good at that!"

Not Robby. He *laughed* and said, "And they want *you* to talk about that?"

Happy Father's Day.

On a more positive note, I had a conversation with one of my *daughters* recently. She told me that she appreciated how Carol and I had raised her. In particular, she liked that we did not just "give her the answer."

We encouraged the kids to handle as much as they could on their own. If they had a problem with a teacher, they needed to talk to that teacher themselves. If they didn't understand something or didn't know the solution to a particular problem, we encouraged them to dig deeper and seek to understand. We would be there to brainstorm and discuss, but we would not do the work for them or give them the answer.

They did not always like it at the time, but as adults, they now appreciate what it did for them.

Daughters are awesome!

Today is the Feast of Corpus Christi, the Body and Blood of Christ.

The thematic readings focus on life-giving bread. From Deuteronomy, we heard, "God fed you with manna, a food unknown to you and your fathers, in order to show you that not by bread alone does one live."

The gospel came from John: "Whoever eats my flesh and drinks my blood has eternal life…For my flesh is true food, and my blood is true drink… This is the bread that came down from heaven."

Just as I taught my own kids, when I seek to understand a particular scripture passage, I dig deeper. I dig into the countless theology books I used in deacon formation. I research online, and I read the scripture that surrounds the passage I am studying.

This allows me to put the scripture in proper context—both sequential and historical. In other words, I gain a deeper understanding of a passage if I know what happened immediately before or after that passage. Studying the historical context allows me to better understand the prevailing culture at the time and answer questions such as "Why did the people respond as they did?"

When I dug deeper into today's readings, I was struck by the strong parallels between the first reading and the gospel:

Each reading referenced a "bread from heaven"—for the Israelites in Deuteronomy, it was manna. It *literally* came from heaven, falling from the sky. For the Jews in the gospel, it was the flesh and blood of Christ. Jesus referred to it as *the bread that came down from heaven.*

In both readings, the bread was new and unlike any bread they had ever seen or experienced before. When the manna fell from the sky, the Israelites initially had no idea what it was or what to do with it.

Obviously, the bread Jesus described to His disciples in the gospel was also new—"For my flesh is true food, and my blood is true drink."

This bread was not only new but very challenging to hear. The Jews would have found this idea extremely repugnant. There were many prohibitions against eating an animal's flesh with its blood; it was strictly forbidden. To say they didn't understand what Jesus was saying is the ultimate understatement.

The parallels between the first reading and the gospel continue in how the Israelites and the Jews *responded* to this new bread being offered to them.

From the Book of Numbers, we know how the Israelites responded: "The people complained against God and Moses, 'Why have you brought us up from Egypt to die in this desert? We are disgusted with this wretched food!'"

So much for the gift of life-changing and life-*saving* food. There was no digging deeper. There was no seeking to understand. There was only rejection.

The Jews' response to Jesus was much the same. If we continue reading John's gospel, we would learn, "Then many of his disciples who were listening said, 'This saying is hard; who can accept it?' As a result of this, many of his disciples returned to their former way of life and no longer accompanied him."

Jesus taught His disciples about the Real Presence in the Eucharist, and as a result we are told, "Many of his disciples returned to their former way of life." They abandoned Him.

Just days earlier, Jesus miraculously fed the five thousand. However, when He tried to get their attention off the physical bread and onto the true Bread of Life, they did not understand. Their response was to turn away.

No digging deeper. No seeking to understand. Only rejection.

Where do these readings lead us? What is the practical application?

The fact is, we are not much different than the Israelites fleeing slavery or the Jews following Jesus.

I once heard chapter 6 of the Gospel of John summarized in this way: "This gospel illustrates the separation of the pretenders from the true disciples."

When challenged by the teachings of Jesus, the pretenders who were along for the ride dispersed. They had been standing on the periphery, taking advantage of what they enjoyed—free food and listening to the new message of love from an exciting new preacher. However, they couldn't commit.

That's modern society. There are many pretenders. They are "all in" until challenged. When they read or hear Church teachings, they cannot fully understand, such as the teachings on the Real Presence in the Eucharist, they respond by saying, "I doubt, or I don't understand, or I don't agree…therefore, I reject."

No digging deeper. No seeking to understand. Only rejection.

Some of these pretenders will leave and add to the growing number of former Catholics or non-churched. Others may not physically leave, but they *will* "return to their former way of life." They will stand on the periphery and take in what they like and reject what they don't like. They will simply go through the motions, picking and choosing.

The bottom line is it's okay to doubt or not understand or not agree. However, our response to these doubts is crucial. We cannot simply *reject*. We must dig deeper. We must ask questions. We must research.

And we don't take a year off to dig deeper. We do so while *continuing* to worship and pray while continuing to be actively engaged in the faith.

In the silence following the homily or in the moments following reception of the Real Presence of Christ in the Eucharist today, I ask that you consider these questions:

- Am I standing on the periphery, picking and choosing what I want to believe or not believe?
- Am I digging deeper and seeking to understand Church teachings that challenge me?
- Am I a pretender?

June 2017

Serve, Pray, Repeat

Thirteenth Sunday in Ordinary Time   2 Kings 4:8–16
                                       Romans 6:3–11
                                       Matthew 10:37–42

I had the honor of speaking to the Serra Club of Indianapolis on Monday evening. The topic was "Our Work is Never Done." The central message of that presentation was, no matter how much you did one day to serve God and others, you are expected to get up the next day and do it again.

One of the reasons many people stray from the Church, or lapse in their faith, is that the role of disciple is demanding and relentless. By nature, human beings are self-centered. To focus on Jesus is hard work and cramps our style.

Scripture does not try to sugarcoat how challenging being a follower of Jesus Christ can be. Today we hear the expectations set before us as Christians. In his letter to the Romans, Paul wrote, "Are you unaware that we who were baptized into Christ Jesus were baptized into his death?" Translation: You live for Christ by dying for Christ.

In Matthew's Gospel, Jesus said, "And whoever does not take up his cross and follow after me is not worthy of me…whoever loses his life for my sake will find it." Translation: You bear the weight of the cross daily…and then you die for Christ.

This description is not the type of job description that has people lining up to apply!

You have likely heard the expression, "If you want something done, ask a busy person." The idea is that those who are busy are busy for a reason. People are constantly asking them to take on more and more because they get results.

Jesus wants us to be busy people. He wants us to work tirelessly on His behalf.

However, it can be exhausting. Carol and I have had several conversations about this over the last few years. We did our job as parents. We work hard, often juggling multiple jobs and outside commitments. We try our best to be good people, nice people. But we get tired. We look into each other's eyes sometimes and can see it: we're drained, and our tanks are empty.

We're at the age when life is supposed to be slowing down, but we're busier now than we've ever been.

So we vent and moan and complain, and then we take a deep breath and pray. We pray first with gratitude, recognizing the many fruits that come from a life of serving God. We pray for perseverance and fortitude and resilience. We pray for the strength to put others first. Then we get up the next day and do it all over again.

I think that's what God wants of us, not the moan and complain part, but the other three steps: Serve others, pray for perseverance, and repeat. Three simple, deliberate, intentional steps.

Like the directions on a shampoo bottle: Lather, rinse, repeat.

Serve, pray, repeat.

Carol came across this timely reflection recently. It reads,

> Did you ever wonder what Jesus meant when He said, "Should anyone press you into service for one mile, go with him for two miles"? (Matthew 5:41).
>
> Jesus wants us to take up a different attitude. Not only should we avoid complaining, but we should be willing to go twice as long as expected—to be generous and serve even beyond what seems reasonable.
>
> That's far easier said than done! When a coworker asks us to work late to help finish a project, it can feel unjust or inconvenient. When

a relative needs help with a home repair late at night, we might want to grumble or delay helping until another day. And when a neighbor asks us to drive an extra carpool during an already busy week, we want to say, "No! Enough already!" We sense we should be more willing, but it's a struggle!

Jesus himself is the best example of going the extra mile. He emptied himself to take on flesh and all our human limitations. He suffered silently and held nothing back when he laid down his life for us. Even now, he never tires of hearing our prayers. He helps us in our weaknesses and forgives us our sins—over and over again.

How can we hope to imitate such generous love? One step at a time.

When we pray, we open the door to God and allow him to renew us. We will find new strength and endurance, greater peace and patience. Just one step and then another. And then another. Add them all up, and we'll find that we have already gone that extra mile. (*Word Among Us*)

This reflection echoes the three steps I just mentioned: Serve, pray, repeat. God knows we're tired, but He needs us and will give us all we need to keep going.

I shared all these thoughts when I spoke to the Serra Club on Monday evening. After my talk, a gentleman approached me and introduced himself. He shook my hand and then held onto it and looked directly into my eyes.

He said, "Deacon Rick, I've never met you, and you've never met me. I'm seventy years old and have only been to a few Serra Club meetings over the last ten years. But I'm on the email list, and I saw the topic of your talk, 'Our Work is Never Done,' so I came to hear what you had to say."

He then shared with me that his wife had gone blind nearly a year ago. He now does everything for her, even though he is older, money is tight, and he needs to continue to work. He cares for his wife before leaving for work. He comes home again at noon to make lunch for her. He returns from work at night and once again tends to his wife.

He said he looks in the mirror at night and almost can't recognize the exhausted and overwhelmed face that is looking back at him. What has kept him going is the love he has for his wife.

Then he ended by saying this: "I believe God sent you here tonight just for me. I needed to hear that what I am doing is God's work. I needed to know why I am being asked to carry this cross. God wants me to be busy doing this work and He'll get me through it."

And he squeezed my hand one more time and said, "And I am going to get up tomorrow and do it again."

I had tears in my eyes. This is what it means to die unto self. This is what it means to "die *with* Christ."

God does not want us to be nailed to a cross and endure a cruel and painful death. He wants us to die unto self. He wants us to fight our natural inclination to be self-centered by putting the needs of others first. He wants us, expects us, to be busy doing His work.

The payoff, according to Paul, is "If, then, we have died with Christ, we believe that we shall also live with him."

God knows we're tired, but He needs us. Pray to Him, and He will give you whatever you need to keep going.

Serve, pray, repeat.

July 2017

I Want to Be Just Like Carol When I Grow Up

Seventeenth Sunday in Ordinary Time	1 Kings 3:5–12
Romans 8:28–30
Matthew 13:44–46

I just returned from a two-week vacation with my wife. While Carol and I live in the same house and work together every day, we don't often get a chance to spend much time with just the two of us. I am thankful for having the past two weeks to reconnect with her.

A thought occurred to me more than once during our vacation: When I grow up, I want to be just like Carol.

I will come back to that thought a little later.

The scripture readings for today were challenging. The first reading left me feeling selfish and petty. The gospel left me feeling confused.

The Old Testament reading was from 1 Kings, and in it, we heard,

> The LORD appeared to Solomon in a dream at night. God said, "Ask something of me and I will give it to you."
> Solomon answered: "Give your servant an understanding heart to judge your people and to distinguish right from wrong."

You may wonder why such a reading would leave me feeling selfish and petty. I tried to imagine for a moment what my response would be if God said the same thing to *me*. How would I respond if God said, "Ask something of me, and I will give it to you?"

I can think of quite a few things that would likely come to mind: a big pile of money, a car with less than 200,000 miles on it, more time for myself, a longer NFL season. As I continue to list things, I might eventually include something for Carol or the kids or the world. However, as ashamed as I am to admit it, the first dozen or so wishes out of my mouth would probably be stuff for *me*. I don't know this for sure, but that's my guess.

Maybe I would surprise myself, and God, and ask for something that would show that I was thinking of others first or thinking of ways to best serve Him. However, I am no Solomon. I can say with some degree of certainty that my response to God would *not* have been to ask for *an understanding heart*. That's an awesome answer.

Solomon gave us something to reflect upon when he responded to God in that way. He did not ask for riches or power or for his enemies to be vanquished. Instead, he asked for an understanding heart, a gift that would make him a better king and a better person. It was a gift he would use to glorify God.

As for the gospel, I mentioned that it left me confused. Confused because it contradicts investment advice I have heard many times over the years. That advice: "Don't put all your eggs in one basket."

It seems like prudent advice. I should not invest all I have in one thing. If that one thing does not pan out, I lose it all.

Today's gospel says just the opposite. Jesus said, "The kingdom of heaven is like a treasure buried in a field, which a person finds and hides again, and out of joy goes and sells all that he has and buys that field."

Sounds like Jesus is telling us to put all our eggs in one basket.

Investment consultants would certainly argue against taking a risk such as this. They would caution us against leaving ourselves so vulnerable.

Jesus tells us that the kingdom of heaven is for those who *allow* themselves to be vulnerable, those who go all in. Full investment in God. All our eggs in His basket.

Two situations occurred while we were on vacation that illustrate the difference between being all in and holding back.

While at poolside, a man entered the area using a walker. Setting the walker aside, he took hold of the handrail and slowly, and painfully, began to lower himself into the pool.

I asked if he needed help and offered to assist him. He politely refused my help.

I was done at that point. I had been nice and offered to assist my fellow man.

Carol went into action. She began by facing him, making eye contact with him, and commenting on how well he was doing. She asked him if the pool was part of his therapy and inquired about his physical condition.

She and John, her new friend, then had a thirty- to forty-minute conversation. John had a stroke very recently. Workouts in the pool helped him strengthen his weakened left side. He was worried about the future and the impact the stroke would have on his job as a teacher with school starting again soon. Carol listened and asked questions. She was engaging, empathetic, and consoling.

I hedged my bet by not totally investing in this man. If he had accepted my offer of help, I would have helped him into the pool and been done. Since he refused my help, at least I had offered, so I was done.

Carol put all her eggs in John's basket, leaving herself completely vulnerable. He could have taken offense at Carol's questions or considered her intrusive, but he didn't. The time spent in conversation with Carol was more therapeutic for him than the water of the pool.

I offered to perform a task for a stranger. Carol offered friendship to John. She had an understanding heart.

Two days later, again under an umbrella at poolside, I sat reading a book while Carol was doing some jewelry making.

A teenage girl was in the pool and at one point came and sat on the edge of the pool near us. She glanced our way a few times. She looked sad and a little lost.

If she had said, "I'm sad, will you comfort me?" I would have gone to her and offered words of support. If she had started crying, I would have gone to her, put an arm around her, and consoled her. But she didn't do either of those things, so I didn't do either of those things. I just read my book and wondered why the girl was sad.

Carol saw the girl glancing our way too. She said, "I'm making some jewelry. Do you want to come over and watch?" The girl, Amy, came over. Carol spent the next hour with her, talking with her and giving her a jewelry-making lesson. They never talked about why Amy was sad, but for that hour, she wasn't.

Carol put all her eggs in Amy's basket and, in so doing, left herself vulnerable. Amy could have given her the teenage girl eye roll or commented that jewelry making was lame, but she didn't.

We found out later from the girl's mom that Amy's best friend had been killed by a drunk driver several weeks ago. The mom thanked Carol for her time. She said while watching Amy make jewelry by the side of the pool, she saw her smile for the first time in a long time.

I was ready to help a young girl if she *asked* for help. Carol stepped in because Amy *might* need help because Carol has an understanding heart.

So while today's readings challenged me—making me feel selfish, petty, and confused—I am now prepared should God come to me in a dream and say, "Ask something of me, and I will give it to you."

Following the example of Solomon, I will ask God for an understanding heart.

I will ask Him if I can be just like Carol when I grow up.

July 2017

Surrender in Faith

Twenty-first Sunday in Ordinary Time	Isaiah 22:19–23
Romans 11:33–36
Matthew 16:13–20

The readings for today caused me to reflect on the age-old question, "How well do you *really* know someone?"

We all have friends we would say we know very well. We claim to understand them; we get where they're coming from. However, they surprise us at times, don't they?

You find yourself in a competitive or stressful or uncomfortable situation with that friend, and they respond differently than you had expected. You walk away from the situation, thinking, "Wow, I thought I knew him better than that."

I have a master's degree in school administration and another master's degree in psychology. I have worked in high schools for twenty-five years. In *theory*, I should know and understand teenagers. And yet, at least once a day, a teenager will do or say something that leads me to believe I know nothing.

I have been married to Carol for thirty-four years. In *theory*, I should know and understand her.

On a regular basis, just when I think I *truly* and *finally* understand her, something happens that leaves me scratching my head.

Are those happy tears or sad tears? Is she upset with something I did or something I didn't do? Something I said or didn't say? That look she is giving me—does it mean I am getting close to crossing the line or that I already crossed it?

My failure to truly understand her is further complicated by the fact that the tears or the look might mean one thing on one day and something completely different the next day.

However, as frustrating as it might be to understand teenagers or my wife, the real energy and growth in the relationship comes from *seeking* to understand.

What does seeking to understand look like?

It requires self-reflection. I have to consider my role in my own frustration. How am I interacting with that teenager? How am I engaging with my wife? Is the way I am participating in this relationship contributing to my lack of understanding?

It requires dialogue—open and honest conversations. I have to be courageous enough to ask tough questions. I won't know if I don't ask. I have to be willing to leave myself vulnerable. By challenging the teen or challenging Carol I risk damaging my relationship with them.

It requires an open heart and an open mind. I must be willing to accept that I don't have all the answers, and that I might never fully understand.

It requires love. The love must be unconditional. I must love through my lack of understanding.

It is critical that I continue to seek understanding. If not, the relationship is dead in the water.

When we consider how incredibly difficult it is to truly know and understand another *human* being, it is not surprising that it is nearly *impossible* to truly know and understand God, the *infinite* and *divine* being.

In his letter to the Romans, Paul voiced a challenge we likely encounter on a daily basis—the challenge of *knowing* God, truly knowing Him. Understanding how He works and what motivates Him. Paul wrote, "How inscrutable are his judgments and how unsearchable his ways!"

Inscrutable means impossible to understand. *Unsearchable* means there is nowhere to find the information that might *help* you to understand.

Given Paul's descriptors, truly knowing God doesn't seem promising. If you're anything like me, each time you feel like you may be *close*, something happens to turn your understanding on its ear.

You know and understand a loving and compassionate God, and then a loved one dies suddenly and unexpectedly.

You know and understand a fair and protective God, and then an earthquake rocks an underdeveloped country like Haiti, killing hundreds of thousands of people and leaving another million or more homeless.

You know and understand a generous God, yet your continued prayers for relief from debt or freedom from addiction seemingly go unheard.

On a recent podcast, Bishop Robert Barron compared our attempt to know and understand God's actions to that of a young child attempting to do the same with his parents.

The young child intuitively *senses* that his parents love him, yet their actions leave him confused.

If they really loved me, would they take me to a doctor and let her stick me with a needle?

If they really loved me, would they put me down for a nap when I would prefer to keep playing?

If they really loved me, would they put up a gate and keep me away from the stairs I would like to explore?

What ultimately happens, Bishop Barron explains, is that the child "surrenders in faith." He accepts the fact that he will not ever fully understand why his parents do what they do, but trusts that it comes from a place of love.

Trust. Faith. Belief in something that the child cannot fully understand.

All this makes the question Jesus asked His disciples in today's gospel come to life: "Who do people say that I am?"

Who do we say You are? We have no idea.

Yet we seek to understand, and the *seeking* becomes the foundation for our faith. It is when we *stop* seeking to understand that the flame of our faith can potentially die out.

Seeking to understand God is no different than seeking to understand our spouse, our children, or our friends.

It requires self-reflection. How am I interacting with God?

It requires dialogue, prayer—open and honest conversations with God.

It requires an open heart and an open mind, accepting that I don't have all the answers.

It requires loving through my lack of understanding.

God constantly reaches out to us. The United States Conference of Catholic Bishops (USCCB) describes His methods in this way: "The methods used by God in reaching out to the world stagger human comprehension but are at the same time a dazzling invitation to abiding faith."

We are obligated to seek understanding.

We are invited to surrender in faith.

August 2017

Direct, Honest, and with Love

Twenty-third Sunday of Ordinary Time	Ezekiel 33:7–9
Romans 13:8–10
Matthew 18:15–20

Speaking for God, the prophet Ezekiel said, "If you do not speak out to dissuade the wicked from his way, I will hold *you* responsible."

Instructing His disciples, Jesus said, "If your brother sins against you, go and tell him his fault."

The readings take us in an interesting direction. Are we being called to judge our fellow man? This certainly is not in line with modern thought. The strong message coming from society is that everyone has a right to do as they please with no moral boundaries.

Being judgmental also flies in the face of foundational Christian ideals—hospitality and welcome to all, celebration of the diversity and unique gifts of others. Didn't Jesus say, "Stop judging, that you may not be judged?"

It is important to note that today's readings focus not on *judging* others but rather on holding others accountable…accountable for their decisions, words, or actions. The readings tell us it is our *responsibility* to hold others accountable. In addition, Jesus told us to be direct in our approach: "If your brother sins against you, go and tell him his fault." *You* go and tell him his fault.

As a high school administrator, I have often used the expression *chain of communication.*

When an issue arises between two people, it is *those two people* who should begin the process of working through that issue. The further apart on the chain we get—the more links between us and the other person—the less effective the communication.

We should not rely on others to do our dirty work. Communicating directly is always best. To do otherwise relegates the issue to hearsay or gossip.

Of course, that is easier said than done. It can be uncomfortable to approach someone about something they have said or done or to call them to task for their actions.

Holding someone else accountable, especially a loved one, is challenging. We don't want to appear to be self-righteous or judgmental. And if you are anything like me, you have enough trouble holding *yourself* accountable, much less anyone else.

For *most* people, it is an uncomfortable thing to do.

I have shared stories about Shirley in the past. Shirley is my elderly neighbor. About eight years ago, I came home on a hot summer day to find Shirley pushing a lawnmower up the incline of a ditch near the street. Although I did not know her well at the time, I was moved to offer her help. I stopped her, told her I would finish mowing her yard, and that her days of cutting grass were over. I told her, and I quote, "You'll never have to worry about your yard again."

Shirley has no problem holding me accountable. I told her she would never have to worry about her yard again, and she holds me to it.

If she feels like her grass is overdue to be mowed, I'll get a phone call from her. After receiving these types of calls on a regular basis, I was frustrated. The frustration came out the next time she called. I was nice, but I pushed back. I assured her that her yard was not that bad. I shared how busy I was and explained that I just hadn't had the time to get it done.

Her response? "Well, I see that you got *your* grass cut."

Ouch! But you know what? She taught me something. She was right. I made a commitment to her and had put my own needs—*my* yard—before hers. Shirley spoke to me directly and held me accountable.

A direct approach comes with risk and makes us uncomfortable. We have no problem with sending a letter to a government official about bad policy or an email to a television station about inappropriate programming. We can even manage critiquing someone who works for us, pointing out areas of their work that need improved.

However, we struggle when it comes to speaking directly to people we care about regarding their behavior. Holding someone accountable is risky.

Telling friends that their drinking or extramarital relationships are damaging and sinful and wrong…and risk losing a friend.

Telling adult children that they are making poor moral decisions or chiding them about not going to Mass…and risk alienation.

Telling spouses that the words they use or the way they treat you is hurtful…and risk receiving an angry, defensive response.

Again, holding someone accountable is risky.

It can also leave you feeling guilty, wondering if you have overstepped your responsibility. There are three simple questions you can ask yourself to determine if you have done the right thing:

One, "Were the behaviors I addressed harmful to that person, to others around him, or to his relationship with God?"

If so, you not only chose to do the right thing but also had an obligation to do so.

Two, "Was my intent to bring that person into right relationship with himself, others, or God?"

This is a critical question, and you need to be honest. You have done the right thing if your intent was pure. You *have not* done the right thing if your intent was to demean or ridicule that person or to assume a stance of moral superiority. Was it about him or about you?

And three, "Was there love in my heart?"

Here is a beautiful definition of love from St. Augustine: Love is willing the good of the other.

If we remain indifferent or uninvolved for fear of hurting someone's feelings, that is not love; that is protecting yourself.

Paul wrote in today's letter to the Romans: "Owe nothing to anyone, except to love one another; for the one who loves another has fulfilled the law."

In other words, if we acted with love in our heart, we did the right thing.

Notice that one of my questions was *not* "Did I get the result I wanted?"

Even if you did everything perfectly, you may not get the result you wanted. You may, in fact, lose a friend, alienate a child, or anger a spouse. As I said, holding those you care about accountable is risky.

However, it's not as risky as *not* holding them accountable. Remember what we heard in the first reading: "If you do not speak out to dissuade the wicked from his way, I will hold *you* responsible."

September 2017

Don't Leave Them Crying on the Field

Thirty-first Sunday of Ordinary Time   Malachi 1:14–2:10
1 Thessalonians 2:7–13
Matthew 23:1–12

I began my illustrious coaching career as a nineteen-year-old, coaching fifth- and sixth-grade CYO football here at St. Pius X. I learned a lot in those early experiences—about football and coaching strategies—but more importantly, about people.

I remember one particular incident that occurred on the practice field. A young man made an error on a play we were attempting to run. I stopped the action on the field. I got eye-to-eye with my young ten-year-old running back, made it clear that an error had been made, and stressed how important it was that he correct that error. I had a moderate increase in the volume and intensity of my voice but nothing alarming. I'm sure my face showed concern, but I am fairly certain it did not show anger. I gave what I felt was a firm and appropriate response, doing my best to correct the error.

In coaching, you learn to watch the eyes for understanding; the eyes tell the story. This young man's eyes came alive. He was encouraged and motivated by my words. He responded enthusiastically, "Yes, Coach! I can do that, Coach!" He then sprinted to the line of scrimmage to show me—to show everyone—that he *could* do it. He ran the play and executed it flawlessly.

Setting humility aside, I remember thinking, "I am a *great* coach, an outstanding motivator of young people!"

The next practice, I had a nearly identical situation with a different player. Confident in my proven abilities, I handled the situation in the identical fashion: eye-to-eye with the young man who had made the mistake. I repeated my performance from the prior day: pointed out the error with a moderate increase in the volume and intensity of my voice, showed a face of concern but not anger, and offered an appropriate response to the situation.

Then I stood back and waited for the magic to happen once again. I watched the young man's eyes to see the fire, to see them come to life.

The eyes *did* tell the story. His eyes immediately filled with tears. In moments, he was sobbing uncontrollably. He took off his helmet and slumped to the ground in the middle of the field. The eyes of all the young athletes and fellow coaches were on me, wondering what I had done to that poor child.

Same error, same technique used to correct the error, and an *entirely* different response.

I learned a valuable lesson that day—a lesson I have reflected upon often as a husband, father, educator, and deacon. Not everyone receives a message the same way. The word choice, volume, and tone used, regardless of content, can impact how different people receive the same message. What works for one person may not work for another.

Lesson learned: You may need to employ a variety of methods to get your point across. In education, we call it differentiated instruction.

Jesus knew that. That's why, at times, he preached about the sanctity of the temple in words and another time, sent this same message by overturning the tables of the moneychangers. Same message, different tone and intensity.

This all came to mind as I prepared this week's homily. I was struggling with the direction to take with these readings. I am not too proud to ask for help, so I asked one of our students, a young man discerning the priesthood, to look over the readings and let me know what stood out to him.

He was happy to do so. He sent me his notes the next day. What struck me most about his response was that it was not directed so much at the content of the readings but more on the tone and intensity of the message.

In the first reading from Malachi, verbiage is direct and demanding: "If you do not listen, if you do not lay it to heart, to give glory to my name, says the LORD of hosts, I will send a curse upon you and on your blessing I will make a curse."

Direct and demanding—"Praise God or else."

In St. Paul's letter to the Thessalonians, we heard a kinder, gentler approach: "We were gentle among you, as a nursing mother cares for her children. With such affection for you, we were determined to share with you the gospel of God…for this reason we give thanks to God unceasingly."

Kinder and gentler—"Join me in praising God."

Finally, the words of Jesus in the Gospel land somewhere in between: "You have but one teacher…you have but one Father in heaven…whoever humbles himself will be exalted."

It's a teaching moment—"Praise God because it is the right thing to do for your salvation."

I have emphasized in the past that sacred scripture is the divinely inspired, personalized word of God. Scripture readings offer to each person an individualized message; each hears what he is intended to hear.

This week's readings take that notion a step farther. Scripture readings also vary the delivery of that message so that it reaches the ears of all.

Why is that important to know?

As Christians, we are called not only to *hear* the message but also to take that message out to the world—to *deliver* the message. We need to be sensitive to our audience and meet people where they are. If we are to be successful in our efforts, we can't rely on only one method of delivery.

Some people need to be *told*: "Praise God."

Some people need to be *invited*: "Join me in praising God."

Some people need to be *taught*: "Praise God because it is the right thing to do for your salvation."

If you are convinced there is only one way to deliver the message and stubbornly lock in to that one method, your message may get through to *some* or even *most* people.

However, you will likely leave others with tears in their eyes, slumped over in the middle of the football field.

November 2017

God's Not Talking to Me, Right?

Thirty-third Sunday of Ordinary Time   Proverbs 31:10–31
1 Thessalonians 5:1–6
Matthew 25:14–30

Carol wanted me to preach on today's first reading from the Book of Proverbs. I'm not sure why, but I did notice a few lines of the reading that might have caught her eye: "When one finds a worthy wife, her value is beyond pearls. Her husband, entrusting his heart to her, has an unfailing prize."

While I agree Carol has value far beyond pearls and is an unfailing prize, I will be focusing on the *other* two readings today.

Have you ever done this? An announcement is being made at work, at school, or at the mall; and after just a few words, you tune it out. You heard something in those first few words that led you to believe the message did not pertain to you.

For instance, the principal at school was on the PA making his morning announcements. He began, "Attention members of the girls swim team." I never heard the rest of that announcement. I am not a girl, nor do I swim. So my brain automatically tuned out the message.

Certainly, there are messages for which we are not the intended audience. They don't pertain to us, so tuning them out is of little consequence.

Other times, the message *is* intended for us, but we don't feel worthy of receiving it. We convince ourselves that the message is for other people, better people, more talented, more successful, or more valued.

We may have been conditioned to believe we are not worthy.

As an athlete, you made a mistake, and the coach ignored it. A more skilled or more talented player made the same mistake, and you heard the coach say, "You have incredible talent! I expect more from you!"

Your perception is, you do *not* have incredible talent, and the coach does not expect more from you.

Maybe as a student, you received a grade of 80 percent on a test. The smarter student to your left received an 80 percent on the test also, and next to the grade was the note, "I am disappointed—you are better than this!"

Your perception is that the teacher was not disappointed in *you* because *you* are *not* better than an 80 percent.

If you are of this mindset, the mindset that says you have little to offer and are mediocre at best, it is possible you tuned out today's gospel. The gospel is clearly intended for the elite; after all, Matthew tells us that the talents were distributed to the servants, *each according to his ability*. The servant with five talents will get five more; the rich get richer.

You do not envision yourself as worthy of five talents; that would be above your pay grade. At best, you see yourself as the servant given one talent; no one expects much from you.

So while others of more value listen to the gospel, you tune it out.

Before we get too caught up in the "I'm not good enough" pity party, I will also ask this challenging question: Are we saying "this message is not for me" or "God is not talking to me" in order to avoid the work He is calling us to? The parable Jesus shared in the gospel clearly says, "I will give you great responsibilities."

To whom much is given, much is expected. God is not talking to *me*.

Great responsibilities? God is not talking to *me*.

Do we really believe God is running a gifted and talented program and handpicking those who are stronger, smarter, and wealthier to be His workers?

Paul must have encountered this "God is not talking to me" mentality in his travels to Thessalonia. Using beautiful language, he clarifies for the Thessalonians, and for us, that God loves all of us, calls all of us, *needs* all of us.

He wrote, "For all of you are children of the light and children of the day. We are not of the night or of darkness. Therefore, let us not sleep as the rest do."

We are not "the rest." We are children of God. We are children of the light.

What a beautiful image in what has become such a dark world. God nudges us—nudges *you*. He asks you, "In this world of darkness, who is going to be the light? Will *you* do this for me?"

We are children of light. It is who we are. It is what we are capable of. It is our identity.

No, not me, we might argue. Jesus said to whom much has been given, much is expected. I'm average; I'm just me, no special gifts or talents. What have I been given?

How about life? How about love—unconditional love from an adoring Father who calls us His children?

No more excuses. You can't get around this call to action. God expects more from *all* of us. He calls us to return to Him what has been given and then some.

We must set aside our feelings of inadequacy. We must stop asking, "What can one average person like me possibly accomplish in a world of darkness?" We must stop saying, "God is not talking to me."

We must use the life we have been given and the unconditional love of God to radiate light and become the children of light we were created to be.

When we accept that challenge, we will hear God's voice echoed in the parable of Jesus: "Well done, my good and faithful servant. Come, share your master's joy."

November 2017

"I'd Make a Great Handmaid!"

Fourth Sunday of Advent	2 Samuel 7:1–16
	Romans 16:25–27
	Luke 1:26–38

If you've been paying attention to the gospel readings for the past two and a half weeks, and I'm sure you have, you may have noticed something.

The gospel reading on the feast of the Immaculate Conception on December 8 was Luke 1:26–38, which ends with these words from Mary: "Behold, I am the handmaid of the Lord. May it be done to me according to your word."

The gospel on December 12, the feast of Our Lady of Guadalupe, was the same—Luke 1:26–38.

On Wednesday of the third week of Advent, this past Wednesday, we read the very same gospel—Luke 1:26–38.

And now, today, celebrating the Fourth Sunday of Advent, we read—you guessed it—Luke 1:26–38 and hear Mary say once again, "Behold, I am the handmaid of the Lord. May it be done to me according to your word."

The Church took a page from the advertising world. The more you repeat the message, the better the result. Repetition leads to recognition, which leads to comfort and familiarity, which leads to buy-in.

The first couple of times, we can understand why this gospel was used. After all, the Immaculate Conception and Our Lady of Guadalupe are Marian feasts; the intent is to celebrate Mary. We celebrate her by highlighting the remarkable selflessness of the words she spoke.

However, the Church offers us this gospel *four* times in a sixteen-day period. The Church is trying to sell us on something. Two times? Maybe it's about Mary. *Four* times? It's about us.

We are offered this gospel four times not only to *hear* Mary's words but also to take them into our hearts. We reflect on the *meaning* of Mary's words. She said her sole purpose for living was to carry out the will of God, *his* will be done, not hers.

Hopefully, after hearing Mary's words four times and reflecting on her beautiful intent, we will choose to imitate her willingness to be a handmaid to God. If not imitate, perhaps we can at least approximate that willingness.

God wants us to be His handmaids. He *needs* us to be His handmaids.

You don't hear the word *handmaids* used much in modern times. Historically and biblically, handmaids generally worked for the wealthy, particularly royalty. By definition, handmaids were those whose sole function was to serve or assist their master. They worked in the trenches, doing the dirty work no one else wanted to do. The will of their master be done, not theirs.

While we may pay laborers to do work we are unable or unwilling to do, we don't have someone at our beck and call, responding to our every need, with the exception of a few lucky pastors who have a deacon assigned to their parish.

Many of us, including myself, take pride in the fact that we *are* willing to do the dirty work. I watch the show *Dirty Jobs* on TV and often say, "I'd be willing to do that!" I would be willing to clean out the inside of a garbage truck or shovel out the stalls at a dairy farm. I am also the guy who is okay with putting away the chairs after an event or pushing a broom when needed.

Maybe this describes you as well. You take pride knowing that no job is beneath you.

You may be thinking, "I would make a great handmaid!" You feel like you can confidently proclaim the same words Mary spoke to the angel, "I am the handmaid of the Lord." His will be done, not mine.

I apologize for bursting your bubble, but there is something you should know. While you are to be commended for your willingness to be a handmaid, God does not likely need you to clean out garbage trucks or shovel out the stalls of dairy farms.

God's dirty work may not actually get you dirty at all. It is dirty work because it is the difficult work, the work no one likes to do, the work that makes us uncomfortable.

Doing God's dirty work means boldly stepping into situations where you see an injustice taking place. It means speaking out on behalf of those who cannot speak for themselves—the unborn, the afflicted, and the disenfranchised.

Doing God's dirty work means rolling up your sleeves to care for the poor and the homeless—praying for them, sharing what you have, dignifying them by looking them in the eye and speaking with them—human being to human being.

Doing God's dirty work means promoting and defending the Church, wearing your faith on your sleeve, and sharing the Good News.

Doing God's dirty work means loving and serving others—serving others before serving ourselves. *His* will be done, not your own.

Being a handmaid for the Lord is not an easy task. Rather than become discouraged by our inability to fully imitate Mary, we can begin by taking small steps toward it.

When I was young, our family would occasionally stay at a hotel as we were traveling on vacation. Before we checked out, my mom always made us clean up the rooms. We made the beds, wiped down the shower and sink, dusted everything off, etc. We—the kids—all moaned and groaned. "Why are we doing this? That is what the maids are for!"

My mom gave the same answer each time: "We should always leave things a little better than we found them."

Perhaps that's where we start: By doing our best to leave the world better than we found it.

Next week, you'll be making a New Year's resolution.

DEACON RICK WAGNER

Why not resolve to start each day by saying, "Your will be done, Lord. Today, I will try to leave things a little better than I find them."

Can you imagine a world in which everyone started his or her day with that frame of mind and then actually lived it out?

December 2017

We Can Never Hear That Story Too Often

Third Sunday in Ordinary Time   Jonah 3:1–10
1 Corinthians 7:29–31
Mark 1:14–20

As the kids were growing up, I missed out on many things while I was at work. When I came home in the evening, I looked forward to being filled in on the events of the day—both the good and the bad.

The kids shared details of the fun events I missed out on, bubbling over with excitement as each shared his or her version of the activities of the day. More often than not, I would hear multiple versions of the same basic story. The characters in the story and the general timeline of events were the same. However, each version of the story, told from a unique perspective, offered slightly different details and focus.

Or perhaps there was a disagreement of some kind. Such disagreements were usually centered around personal property, invasion of space, or some other issue critically important to children.

I would hear both sides of the disagreement. Both children were victims, of course, and no one was ever at fault. Then Carol would weigh in with her take on the squabble. No one's version was wrong or dishonest; each was simply telling the story from his or her own perspective.

This idea of multiple versions of the same story came to mind as I read today's gospel.

I read Mark's gospel story of Andrew and Peter being called as disciples and said to myself, "Wait a minute…didn't we hear this same story *last week*?" It wasn't the same Gospel reading but the same story.

I double-checked, and sure enough, last Sunday we heard *John's* version of this very same story—Jesus calling Andrew and Peter to be disciples.

This raised two questions: First, why are there two different gospels offering the same basic story? And second, the broader question, why did theologians and scholars bother to include *four* gospels in the New Testament with multiple versions of many of the same stories?

The answer to both questions is *perspective* and *focus*.

In John's gospel last week, Andrew heard John the Baptist refer to Jesus as the Lamb of God. Andrew then listened to Jesus speak for a time and was convinced He was the Messiah. He ran and got his brother, Peter, and brought him to Jesus and both Andrew and Peter were called to be disciples.

In Mark's gospel today, we have the same characters and same basic timeline, but the details included in the telling of the story give it a different focus.

Jesus came across fishermen Andrew and Peter as He passed the Sea of Galilee. He called them with the simple message of "Come after me, and I will make you fishers of men." We are told Andrew and Peter "abandoned their nets and followed him."

John emphasized Jesus as Lord and focused on the honor of being called to be a disciple of Jesus.

Mark emphasized Andrew and Peter's response to the call, a response that showed an immediate and unwavering faith. Notice they did not pack up their nets and place them neatly in their boat. They did not tie up their boat and cover it until they returned. The emphasis is on the details. We are told they *abandoned* their nets. They never planned to return to their former life again. Following Jesus was their new vocation, and they were all in.

Two perspectives on the same story. John's details focus on Jesus and the call. Mark's details focus on Andrew and Peter and their response.

As to our second question, the broader question, why are *four* gospels included in the New Testament?

The naïve thought might be that there were only four gospels available, so those charged with compiling scripture decided to keep all four to make it easier. The fact is, at the time the canon of the New Testament was assembled, over *fifty* gospels had been written. Rather than choose one, they were inspired by God to choose four gospels. Those four gospels gave the reader four different perspectives and focused on different aspects of Jesus, His ministry, and His followers.

Matthew, writing to a Jewish audience, emphasized Jesus as the fulfillment of Old Testament prophecy, Jesus as the long-awaited Messiah.

Luke portrayed Jesus as the answer to the world's problems, emphasizing His perfect humanity and His concern for the weak, the suffering, and the outcast.

As for the two gospel writers we are discussing today, John emphasized the divinity of Jesus. His gospel was written with the specific purpose of providing us with a foundation for our trust in Jesus—to give us confidence. In the story of the calling of Andrew and Peter, we hear John the Baptist announce Jesus as the Lamb of God, and we recognize that we can trust Him when we are called.

Mark's gospel portrays Jesus as a servant, one willing to suffer and die for the good of others. More importantly, perhaps, it emphasizes that we, too, must be servants. We are called to be disciples of Jesus, people who are willing to follow His example. Thus, in today's Gospel, Jesus said to Andrew and Peter, "Come after me"; and they immediately abandoned their nets and followed Him.

When listening to my kids recap their day, I would never have listened to only one child's version. I would never have said to the second child, "Don't bother telling me, I already know the story." The second child had a unique perspective. Each version of the story had its own purpose and value.

When we hear a familiar gospel story, we shouldn't tune out by saying, "I already know that story." We listen for the purpose of the author. We value the perspective offered. We listen carefully to the details. What does the gospel writer, what does *God*, want us to hear?

Last week, God wanted us to know, from John's perspective, that we can trust in His Son's call.

Knowing we can trust in His Son's call, today God wants us to know, from Mark's perspective, that we must respond. We must abandon our nets and leave our former life behind. We must be all in.

We can never hear that story too often.

January 2018

It's Okay to Pick Up Tommy's Tie

Sixth Sunday in Ordinary Time   Leviticus 13:1–2, 44–46
1 Corinthians 10:31–11:1
Mark 1:40–45

When I was in second grade, right here at St. Pius, the time came for my class to prepare for receiving our First Holy Communion. We practiced each day in the church, which is now Ross Hall. We were informed of all the dos and don'ts of our big day. The girls must wear white dresses and wear veils. The boys must wear dress shirts and sport coats and little clip-on ties. We were to walk in a straight line with our hands folded. There was to be *no* slouching.

A major emphasis, at least as far as Sr. Antoinette was concerned, was that we stay focused. That meant we were not to look around trying to find our parents or grandparents. We were not to look out the window. We were not to talk to anyone for any reason, except to say "Amen" when Msgr. Ross offered us Holy Communion.

Sr. Antoinette was so passionate about us paying attention that she gave what I thought was a very odd example. She said, "Even if someone's veil or tie falls off, you must continue to look straight ahead."

I remember thinking what a strange example that was. I could imagine a veil falling off, but when has someone's tie ever fallen off?

Fast forward to the day of our First Holy Communion. We were all dressed as instructed. We processed in with hands folded and walking in a very straight line. I was sitting next to one of my best friends, Tommy McKay, but I assured my mom that I would not misbehave.

I was paying attention. I was focused. I was following the rules.

And then it happened. I saw it out of the corner of my eye. Tommy's tie fell off.

I panicked. *I* saw his tie fall off, but Tommy *did not* see it. Poor guy was tieless. I looked around quickly; no one was looking in my direction. Sister's warning was ringing in my ears: "Even if someone's tie falls off…" I bent down and picked up the tie.

I tapped Tommy on the shoulder. Despite explicit instructions not to talk to anyone for any reason, I whispered to him, "Your tie fell off."

There I was, an eight-year-old dedicated rule-follower who had broken the rules not once but twice. I was petrified. I quickly looked over at Sr. Antoinette, hoping she hadn't seen me.

She *had* seen me, but for some strange reason, she was smiling.

Hold on to that thought.

Sometimes, I read one of the Old Testament selections and wonder, "How does this reading contribute to my understanding of God or my faith?"

For example, today's first reading. To put the reading into context, it comes from the chapters of Leviticus dealing with the laws of purity. What we heard today were the rules for those afflicted with leprosy.

We heard in the reading, "The one who bears the sore of leprosy shall keep his garments rent and his head bare, and shall muffle his beard; he shall cry out, 'Unclean, unclean!' He shall dwell apart, making his abode outside the camp."

The "leper rules" were clearly laid out; they explained what the *leper* must do. If we were to read further in Leviticus, we would hear more about how *others* should *treat* lepers. One must not touch a leper or his garments or even enter an area where a leper has been quarantined, or that person will be deemed unclean as well.

While this might be interesting information historically or even medically, what relevance does it have for us?

Here is the twist: In the first reading, we heard all the rules for dealing with leprosy—how to *live* as a leper as well as the need for others to avoid *contacting* a leper. Then in the gospel, all those rules were thrown out the window, completely disregarded by both the leper *and* Jesus.

The rule said a leper must stay away from others and must cry out "Unclean!" if anyone were to approach. Yet the gospel says the leper came to Jesus and knelt down right in front of Him—an obvious disregard for the established law.

Rather than correct the behavior, Jesus compounded the misdeed by disregarding the law as well. We heard, "Moved with pity, Jesus stretched out his hand, *touched* him, and said, 'Be made clean.'" He *touched* the leper.

After the leper had been made clean, Jesus told him, "See that you tell no one anything." The leper completely ignored this as we are told in the gospel: "The man went away and began to publicize the whole matter."

The rule was, lepers must not approach anyone. The leper approached Jesus.

The rule was, never touch a leper. Jesus touched the leper.

The rule was, don't tell anyone about this. The leper told everyone he saw.

Not even *Jesus* followed the rules.

However, if you think about it, Jesus was not exactly the poster child for rule-following; just ask the Pharisees. How many times in the gospels do we hear the Pharisees questioning Jesus about His lack of adherence to the law? Why does He heal on the Sabbath? Why does He not ritually wash His hands before eating? Why does He eat with sinners and prostitutes?

Which brings me back to my initial question, "How do these readings contribute to my understanding of God or my faith?"

Are the readings promoting anarchy? Is the takeaway supposed to be *rules are meant to be broken?*

The first reading detailed the rules. The gospel showed the rules being broken. It is in the second reading that we get the message that ties it all together. From Paul, we heard, "Do everything for the glory of God…not seeking your own benefit but that of the many, that they may be saved."

Jesus was not about following rules *or* breaking rules; He was about glorifying God. He was about benefiting the many so that they may be saved.

When the leper broke the rules and approached Jesus, he showed incredible faith. He *knew* in his heart that Jesus could cure him. In expressing that faith so intentionally and with such conviction, he was glorifying God.

Jesus broke the rules when he touched the leper. We were told that Jesus was *moved with pity*. By allowing His heart to be moved with pity, by acting with compassion, He was glorifying God.

The former leper *went away and began to publicize the whole matter* despite what Jesus had told him. He broke the rules. However, in singing the praises of Jesus and spreading the news of the miraculous healing, he was glorifying God.

Do everything for the glory of God…not seeking your own benefit but that of the many.

I will continue to be a rule-follower. However, I know that there will be times when our hearts fill with pity, and we act out of compassion for the benefit of others.

At those times, it is okay to touch the leper.

At those times, it is okay to pick up Tommy's tie.

February 2018

Why Aren't We Angry?

Third Sunday of Lent

Exodus 20:1–17
1 Corinthians 1:22–25
John 2:13–25

How many times did we hear this gospel in religion classes as we were growing up? It was read to us anytime we were studying the humanity of Jesus. "He had all the same feelings and emotions that we do," the teacher would say. "Jesus had friends. He hugged his mother. He cried. He was joyful. *And…*Jesus got *angry.*"

We would gasp at this revelation. What?! Jesus got mad?

Then the teacher would read the story of the cleansing of the temple we heard today:

> Jesus made a whip out of cords and drove them all out of the temple, and spilled the coins of the money changers and overturned their tables, and to those who sold doves he said, "Take these out of here, and stop making my Father's house a marketplace." His disciples recalled the words of Scripture, "Zeal for your house will consume me."

My teacher explained that Jesus didn't get angry like *we* get angry. She called it "righteous indignation."

It brought to mind the times I chased my little brother and his friends out of my room with a plastic sword, and those times I flipped over a board game I was playing with my sister because I didn't like the outcome.

I know it was anger that caused those behaviors. I also know that if I tried to tell my parents that I had done it out of "zeal for my house" or "righteous indignation," my punishment would have been even worse.

This familiar gospel story raises questions for our consideration:

- Why was Jesus so angry?
- Why were His actions not sinful?
- Is it ever okay for *us* to get angry?

To begin, why *was* Jesus so angry? Let's look first at what the temple was intended to be then visualize what it had become.

The temple for the Jewish people was the very dwelling place of God on earth, the place where heaven and earth met. It was the place where harmony between divinity and humanity was achieved, where the one true God was honored and worshipped. It was a sacred house of prayer, especially during the time of Passover, the height of the Jewish year.

Keeping that in mind, Jesus encountered not a house of prayer, not a sacred place, but a marketplace. Listen to this historical description of what Jesus would have seen and heard in the temple:

> There was a roaring trade in sacrificial animals in the great courtyard of the temple. The demand for pure, sacrificial animals was huge, so at the temple, one would have heard a symphony of animals braying, birds screeching, the stench of living and dying animals, the carnage from the slaughtered sacrifices, and the reverberating sound of animal traders and money changers hawking their wares.

What Jesus encountered was *not* coffee and doughnuts in the narthex. It was sacrilegious chaos. It was not only physically dirty; it was spiritually and ethically dirty. The temple was in need of cleansing. *That's* why Jesus was angry.

Listen again to how He acted on His anger: "He made a whip out of cords and drove them all out of the temple...spilled the coins of the money changers and overturned their tables."

Which brings us to question #2: Why were His actions *not* sinful? If we find truth in our Church documents, we know Jesus *did not* sin.

In the Vatican document, *Gaudium et Spes* [*Joy and Hope*], we read, "The Son of God worked with human hands, He thought with a human mind, acted by human choice and loved with a human heart. He has truly been made one of us, like us in all things except sin."

He is like us in all things except sin.

If we accept Jesus was without sin, we must look at His actions in the temple that day through a different lens. We must look at His motivation and intent. Perhaps it is easiest to go back to the simple explanation of the religion teacher I mentioned earlier, who told us Jesus didn't get angry like *we* get angry; His anger was "righteous indignation."

Let's compare *our* anger to that of Jesus. We generally get angry when someone offends us or keeps us from doing something we want to do. We get angry when we want something for ourselves but don't get it. In other words, our anger is most often centered on ourselves and our desires.

In comparison, Jesus was angry because the actions of those in the temple offended *God*. He was angry because the merchants were treating God's house with contempt. They were cheating the people who came to worship and manipulating sacrificial law to benefit themselves. Instead of a selfish anger, Jesus acted out of a righteous anger. The anger of Jesus wasn't self-directed; he defended the holiness of his Father's temple.

That speaks to motivation; what about intent? For Jesus, intent was clear: Right the wrong and send a message. By cleansing the temple, He restored its sacred purpose. He also sent a powerful message for all to hear: "Stop making my Father's house a marketplace."

Our intent is much less noble. We generally operate on payback: "Someone hurt me or offended me, so I will do the same in return." Our anger is prideful. Our anger is centered on self. As a matter of fact, we are more likely to get angry over a minor inconvenience to ourselves than a grievous injustice done to others. Such anger is sinful.

This leads us to our final question: Is it *ever okay* for us to get angry?

The short answer is, "Yes, absolutely!" As a matter of fact, Catholic social teaching calls us to anger when we see God's kingdom under attack, when we see the dignity of life disregarded, when we see those most vulnerable enduring neglect and abuse, when grave sin is flaunted before us, and when we witness evil that profanes God's holiness. Absolutely, we should be angry, and we should act on that anger.

This anger should be a righteous anger focused on what offends God. It should be an anger governed by love, directed not at people, but at the actions that are offensive. We are not perfect. Our actions offend God at times too. So peace and compassion must be a part of our righteous anger.

Channel the anger into something productive. *Sometimes*, righteous anger translates into fashioning whips out of cords and turning over tables—*but not always*. Sometimes, it is praying for those whose actions have offended God. Sometimes, it is pulling aside a family member or friend who is on the wrong path and offering guidance and encouragement. Sometimes, it is writing a letter to government officials who have the power to change how things are done. Sometimes, it is holding a sign outside of Planned Parenthood. Sometimes, it is handing a sandwich to someone who is hungry.

Jesus was like us in all things but sin, which means we have the ability to be *like Him* in all things. Many temples in our world need cleansed. Why aren't we angry? And if we *are* angry, why are we not *acting* on that anger?

March 2018

Go Ahead and Jump

Second Sunday of Easter   Act 4:32–35
                                1 John 5:1–6
                                John 20:19–31

I once saw a single-frame comic in a Christian magazine in the doctor's office. It came to mind when reflecting on today's gospel reading. The comic showed the apostles sitting in a large room, watching television together. On the TV screen was a show in which one of the characters, with drooping shoulders and a sad face, was saying, "I'm sorry for being such a Doubting Thomas."

The apostles in the comic were all having a great laugh, slapping their knees with delight and pointing at Thomas. Thomas was red in the face, and steam was coming out of his ears. A thought bubble was over his head that read, "You make *one* mistake and you never hear the end of it."

His famous mistake: "Unless I see the mark of the nails in his hands and put my finger into the nail marks…I will not believe."

Poor Thomas—a victim of poor timing and circumstances! He was *not* in the right place at the right time and has forever been branded as Doubting Thomas.

The fact is, it is very likely that any one of the other apostles would have had the same response. We could just as easily be using the phrase Doubting James or Doubting Andrew in our everyday language.

All disciples of Jesus doubted at one time or another. Many doubted Jesus right to His face. Earlier this week, we heard the familiar gospel story of the Road to Emmaus. Cleopas had a conversation with the risen Jesus that lasted hours, yet he never recognized Jesus. Was Jesus a master of disguise?

No, but Cleopas *saw* Him crucified. He was there when nails were driven into His hands and feet. He watched the soldier pierce His side. He heard Jesus say, "It is finished." He watched the lifeless body taken down from the cross and saw Mary mourn the loss of her son.

So when Cleopas met Jesus on the road to Emmaus he didn't recognize Him. Not because Jesus looked different or wore a disguise but because he didn't believe Jesus had risen from the dead. Despite the fact that Jesus had told His disciples He would come again in glory and would be with them again, Cleopas doubted.

Mary Magdalene, friend and disciple, saw the risen Jesus as well. She assumed she was talking with the gardener. Was Jesus pulling weeds or tilling the soil? No, she didn't recognize Jesus because she didn't believe He would rise from the dead. That couldn't be Jesus because Jesus was dead. She came to the tomb to anoint the dead body of her friend. She doubted what Jesus had told her.

If we really want to point our fingers at a professional doubter, we have to look no further than Peter—lead apostle and eventual first pope of the Church. Jesus told the disciples that He must go to Jerusalem and suffer greatly from the elders, the chief priests, and the scribes; be killed; and on the third day be raised. Peter responded by saying, "No such thing shall ever happen to you!" He, too, expressed doubt.

While Doubting Cleopas or Mary or Peter may not have the same ring as Doubting Thomas, all had their doubts. *All* of Jesus's followers doubted.

So we should be cautious in judging Thomas. When we look in the mirror, we may look just like him.

How often have we thought to ourselves, "Yeah, I'll believe that when I see it" when it comes to our relationship with God? And what is doubt other than a lack of trust? A lack of faith?

We know what God can do for us. We know of His power and His love for us. We talk the talk, saying things like, "All things are possible with God." Yet still we doubt.

We find it very difficult to leave situations in God's hands. As much as we claim to be a people of faith, doubt creeps in when difficult times arise. We step to the edge of the cliff and are afraid to jump despite knowing God is waiting to catch us. Rather than rely on our faith, we, like Thomas, fall into the trap of "show me" or "prove it."

We have become a society of skeptics, a Church of doubters.

Here is data from one diocese in New England, compiled in a study following infants baptized in the faith. In 2002, there were 1,514 infant baptisms in the diocese. In 2010, 999 of those baptized received first Communion. In 2017, 625 of them were confirmed. That means nearly 60 percent of those young people, or the parents charged with raising them in the faith, experienced doubt—enough doubt that they cut ties with the Church or, at the very least, allowed their faith to lie dormant.

We may be thinking, "Not me, Lord! I would never doubt you!"

Every time we turn away from God in our greatest need, rather than *run* toward Him, we doubt.

Every time we choose *things*—money, popularity, power—over God, we doubt.

Every time we refuse to listen to the voice of God because it is uncomfortable to hear, we doubt.

When we skip Mass or cut prayer from our busy day or refuse to reach out to someone who needs us, we are making a statement. We are saying, "I have things to do that are more important than growing my relationship with God." It is a self-centered statement. It is a statement that, at its core, expresses doubt. After all, if we truly believe in the risen Christ and know of His unconditional love for us, how could *anything* be more important?

Placing our trust in God, fighting *against* doubt, is challenging. However, it is a battle worth fighting.

At a deacon's retreat I attended yesterday, Fr. Pat Beidelman described what it was like for him when trust began to replace doubt. He said, "I have experienced so much of His power, His faithfulness, and His love in my life that now it feels less like jumping off a cliff into the unknown and more like returning to a warm and familiar place."

Doubt, the fear of jumping off a cliff, was replaced by trust and a warm and familiar place.

Imagine what could be accomplished if we, as a faith community, were all on the same page in this regard. We heard what that might be like in our first reading from the Acts of the Apostles: "The community of believers was of one heart and mind…with great power the apostles bore witness to the resurrection of the Lord Jesus, and great favor was accorded them all."

In other words, go ahead and jump.

April 2018

Where Has Our Sense of Awe Gone?

Fifth Sunday of Easter   Acts 9:26–31
                              1 John 3:18–24
                              John 15:1–8

I saw a different side of Fr. Jim last Saturday night at Mass. Pacer star Victor Oladipo was at that Mass and was standing in the back of the church. During the singing of the "Alleluia" verse, he made his way to the front to find a seat. So he was walking down the main aisle just as I was going to Father to receive my blessing to read the gospel.

The blessing goes like this: "May the Lord be in your heart and on your lips, that you may proclaim his Gospel worthily and well, in the name of the Father, Son, and Holy Spirit."

This is what Fr. Jim said, "Bless…um…" He finally snapped out of it, gave the blessing, and said, "Sorry, I was distracted."

He called it distracted. Fr. Jim was starstruck!

This led me to wonder if the reverse would be true—if Victor would be distracted if Fr. Jim walked into the arena. As a precaution, I've asked Father not to attend any Pacer games, or at least not during the playoffs.

I am not sharing this story *only* to poke fun at Fr. Jim, although that is a secondary benefit. The story also fits in well with the overall theme of my homily.

Here is a brief summary of the first reading from the Acts of the Apostles: "The church was at peace. It was being built up…and it grew in numbers."

And from the Gospel of John: "Jesus said: 'My Father is the vine grower. He takes away every branch in me that does not bear fruit.'"

So the takeaway from today's readings: We bear fruit when we build up the Church.

The readings of the entire Easter season are focused on the apostles' efforts to share the good news, the joy of the Resurrection. Their actions allowed for the building up of the Church, with the number of Christians growing from those eleven men to the 2.3 billion believers in the world today.

The apostles were sent out to bear fruit, to grow the Church. They did this by sharing their personal experience of the risen Christ.

All Christians have that same responsibility.

While that 2.3 billion number certainly sounds impressive, it is a number that has remained flat in recent years and has even declined in many areas of the world. Even sadder, our world has become increasingly more secular with many having no belief in God at all.

The number of nonbelievers worldwide is at 1.3 billion and growing rapidly. Approximately 25 percent of American adults claim no religious affiliation. We are becoming a godless world, and it shows.

So what can *we* do about it? Well, for starters, we can take the directives from today's readings seriously. We can bear fruit by growing the church.

The manner in which we do this will be different than it was for the original apostles, but the bottom line is the same—we share our experience of Christ. We tell our story. We share with others the awe and wonder of God's presence in our lives.

I assisted at the First Communion Masses here at St. Pius yesterday. Fr. Jim had the kids come forward to sit on the steps and help him with the homily. Each time he asked a question, their hands shot into the air. They couldn't wait to share what they knew about Jesus.

Later, the excitement and reverence with which the children put out their hands to receive the Body of Christ was inspiring. I saw firsthand the awe and wonder of their initial encounter with Christ in the Eucharist.

What has happened to *our* sense of awe? Where has it gone? Are we no longer appreciative or even aware of God's presence in our daily lives? Are we no longer starstruck or distracted by God? Does God no longer amaze us?

Or has our sense of awe been highjacked? Do we only experience beauty, fascination, and amazement in worldly things? Have we become *that* secular?

God is active in our lives. I believe He still elicits a sense of awe and wonder for us. In my heart, I know God is still relevant. I believe He is still important to people and truly impacts their lives.

The problem is, we don't share our experiences. We keep them to ourselves as if we are not allowed to talk about them.

I'm as guilty of this as anyone. For instance, when I went home after Mass last Saturday, I told several people about my encounter with Victor Oladipo and told *no one* about my encounter with Christ in the Eucharist.

I once made it a point to talk to my son at length about a YouTube video of a cat turning a light switch on and off. However, the other night, when I took the trash out, there was a full moon and a slight breeze in the air. The moonlight came through the trees and left a shadow on our porch. I stood and took it all in. I took a moment to pray in gratitude for that moment in time, that epiphany moment when God revealed Himself to me through the beauty of His creation. However, I shared that moment with no one until now.

I am in a position professionally to share my faith on a regular basis. I help with retreats, I do public speaking, and I deliver homilies here at the parish and at school. I use those opportunities to share my personal experience of Christ and stories of God revealing Himself to me.

However, in my one-on-one encounters with the people I see every day, faith rarely comes up in conversation.

During a break in your workday, you find yourself chatting for a few minutes with a coworker. How often is that time spent mindlessly discussing the weather? What would happen if you said, "I was going to take a moment to pray, would you like to join me?"

When you go to a party with friends, you discuss jobs, sports, movies, the kids…even politics. How often do you hear anyone say, "You won't believe how God touched my life today" or "Let me share how God revealed Himself to me today?"

When you sit down with your kids for dinner, you ask them about the highs and lows of their day. You hear about recess, a good grade on a paper, and how someone got sick in gym class. What if you asked a different question like "Where did you see God today?"

Why are we so hesitant to talk openly about our experience of God? What are we afraid of? Are we afraid of what people will think? And what *will* they think…that we love God? That we are proud of our faith? What is the downside?

Perhaps, like many people, you use the excuse "I don't talk about my faith. It is personal." Faith *is* personal, but it is not private; it is intended to be shared.

Like you, my relationship with Jesus Christ is unique. No one's relationship—no one's faith—is exactly like mine. That makes it personal. However, that does not give me permission to keep it to myself. I am called to share my faith.

There is nothing wrong with being distracted by a star athlete. There is nothing wrong with talking about the weather, or movies, or the kids…or even about cat videos. But your experience of Christ, your faith story, should be included in your conversations.

It is those conversations that will bear fruit and build up the Church.

April 2018

Motherly Advice

Feast of the Ascension of the Lord (and Mother's Day!)

Acts of the Apostles 1:1–11

Ephesians 4:1–7, 11–13

Mark 16:15–20

I have often heard people refer to scripture as an instruction manual. While I understand what they mean by that, I find that image to be somewhat cold and impersonal. I don't want to find the Bible in the "how-to" section of my local library.

Scripture is the divinely inspired word of God. I want the word of God to be for me. I want it to talk to me directly and personally. I want it to inspire me and make me a better person.

In a reflection I read recently, a woman wrote that she turns to scripture for advice. I like that. It gives more of a pull-up-a-chair-and-let's-talk-about-it feeling to scripture. It makes it personal. Although we may both pull up chairs to the same scripture, we will *individually* get the advice we need to hear. Advice that inspires and makes me want to be a better person.

The idea of scripture as a source of advice fits in well with our readings for today.

We begin the final week of the Easter season. Over the last six weeks, we have celebrated the joy and hope of the Resurrection. The scripture we heard over the Easter season emphasized God's unconditional love for us. Readings from the Acts of the Apostles detailed the sadness the apostles felt following the death of their friend, Jesus. This sadness turned to joy and hope when He returned to them.

Next week, we'll celebrate Pentecost. Once the apostles receive the gift of the Holy Spirit, they will have the tools they need to get started. They will roll up their sleeves and get to work.

That's where we've been and where we're headed next week. Where are we now? With the Feast of the Ascension, we find ourselves in between the joy and hope of the Easter season and the Holy Spirit driven determination of Pentecost.

For the apostles, it was a time of hesitation, a period of time in which they felt unworthy and ill-equipped to do what was being asked of them. In the first reading, the apostles were left, literally, "standing there looking at the sky." They watched as the physical body of Jesus was taken from their midst forever. They were frozen in their tracks. The obvious question emerged, "Now what?"

They needed advice.

These particular readings and the idea of scripture as a source of inspiring advice come at a perfect time. After all, it is Mother's Day. Other than God, who gives better advice than a mom?

This gave me an idea. I decided to reach out to my kids and ask them to share with me the best advice they had ever gotten from their mom (my wife). Not only will this help me make a point in my homily, Carol will also see it as a sweet gesture from me, making it a very inexpensive Mother's Day gift.

Here are their responses:

"The best advice I ever got from mom was that everyone has a story to tell, and one of the best things we can do is *listen* to their story."

"When I was little, I remember asking Mom who she loved the most. She said, 'Your dad.' (That's me!) I was surprised. I guess I was expecting her to say she loved *me* best or she loved us all equally. She added, 'The best way to love you guys is to love Daddy.' As confusing as it was at the time, now that I'm a dad, it is something I keep close to my heart. I know when I love my wife, I am loving my kids."

"When we had our first child, Mom told me, 'Trust your instincts. No one in the world knows your baby like you do.' Remembering those words has given me more confidence as a mom."

"Mom taught me that a Noble Romans personal pan pizza is the cure for whatever ails you. I have taken that advice very seriously over the years."

Other than the last one, I was moved by their heartfelt responses. Carol's advice was never given as a "do this, or you'll fail" directive. It was given as something to think about and reflect upon. It was meant to be held in their hearts and used as needed. It was meant to inspire.

Have our kids *always* followed Carol's advice? Probably not, but when they didn't, I'm sure her words came to mind, and they heard her voice whispering that same advice in their ear.

Paul's letter to the Ephesians is full of "motherly" advice: "Live in a manner worthy of the calling you have received. Live with "*humility and gentleness.*" Live "*with patience, bearing with one another through love.*"

Paul recognized that the people of Ephesus were hesitant. They were, in effect, doing what the apostles at the ascension had done—standing there looking at the sky. Jesus was no longer there to teach them and walk with them on their journey of faith.

So Paul offered his advice on how they should conduct themselves: Be humble and gentle, be patient, and love one another.

Many pieces of advice and none were delivered as a directive. It was not presented as "do this, or else." Rather, something to think about and reflect upon, something to inspire, advice to be held in their hearts and used as needed.

Finally, in Mark's gospel, while the apostles did not fully understand, Jesus had made it clear that the time would come when He would leave them. So the apostles asked Jesus what they should do after He was gone. He offered this advice: "Go into the whole world and proclaim the gospel to every creature."

Scripture whispers reminders in our ear. Its words of advice urge us to reach for holiness. The advice is not threatening but rather encouraging and meant to be held in our hearts.

Just like Carol's advice to the kids, scripture presents us with the ultimate goal. We should continually strive to reach that goal. Acknowledging we are human beings and will never be perfect, we work to *approximate* the goal.

Chances are, we will never reach the ultimate goal while here on earth. We will never live as God calls us to live all day every day, and that's why we have Reconciliation. However, we will get much *closer* to the goal if we are constantly *striving* to reach it, rather than dismissing it as unattainable.

In other words, our kids may not always follow Carol's advice. They may not *always* listen to the stories of others or love their spouse like they should, but how often *will* they do it if *always* is their goal?

We may not *always* be gentle and patient as Paul suggests, but how often could we *be* gentle and patient if *always* was our goal?

Finally, we may not be able to proclaim the gospel to *every* creature, but how many creatures *would* hear the gospel if *every* creature was our goal?

May 2018

Embrace the Mystery of the Trinity

Solemnity of the Most Holy Trinity   Deuteronomy 4:32–34, 39–40
Romans 8:14–17
Matthew 28:16–20

A priest was presenting to a group of second graders preparing to receive their first holy Communion. He shared the Church's teaching on the Real Presence of Jesus in the Eucharist. He was, of course, bombarded with questions: "Is it like magic? How does Jesus fit in the host? How is Jesus in all the hosts at the same time?"

Finally, the priest said, "It is one of the mysteries of the Church." He should have stopped there, but he made the mistake of adding, "Just like the Trinity is a mystery."

This, of course, led to "What's the Trinity?" The priest did his best to simplify the concept of the Trinity for the eight-year-olds. Hands shot up into the air: "So is *that* like magic? Who's in charge when all three of them are together? How can the Father be the Son? My grandma says, 'Holy Ghost'—is the Holy Ghost God too?"

Exasperated, the priest did his best to return to his "mystery" response. He told them, "These are all good questions. That's why we refer to these things as mysteries. A mystery of the Church is unable to be understood by the human mind."

This answer seemed to impress the kids as well as quiet them.

The priest took advantage of the quiet and attempted to end his presentation. "Are there any other questions?" he asked cautiously.

One hand went up, and a boy asked, "Last week, you said that Jesus was God *and* human, right?"

The priest smiled, delighted that someone had remembered one thing he had taught them.

"Yes, that's right," he answered. "Human—like us in all things but sin."

The little boy asked, "So does *Jesus* understand the Trinity?"

I remember the course we took on the Trinity during the third year of my deacon formation. At the end of the final session, the sixteen of us were dazed and confused, even disoriented. The Trinity is a mind-blowing theological concept. We had difficulty wrapping our minds around all we had read and heard. The thought that parishioners might come to *us* to help them understand the Trinity left us unsettled. At the conclusion of the course, it remained a *mystery*.

There are three nuggets I've heard over the years that have helped me to experience the Trinity. Not understand the Trinity but experience it.

First, since I gave Fr. Jim a hard time a few weeks ago, I will give him credit where credit is due. And now is a great time to do that because he's out of town, and it won't go to his head.

This came from Fr. Jim in a past homily: "The Trinity is a mystery to behold, not to be solved."

I get a sense of relief from those words. It is like being told by a math teacher that is not important to *solve* the equation; the real knowledge comes from *working on it*.

In past homilies, I have stated that *not* understanding certain aspects of our faith, or even *doubting* or *questioning* them, is acceptable. I think that sentiment bears repeating.

Doubt is okay. It is a very human response. The key is in how we address our doubt. The easy path is to simply reject what we don't understand. That is the path chosen by so many who have left the Church.

We should not stop seeking to understand, but it should not consume us. It is always worthwhile to spend time studying, digging into, and asking questions about our God and our faith. Such efforts keep us engaged and active, but we should be careful. We should not get so caught up in trying to *understand* the Trinity that we do not *appreciate* the Trinity.

In today's gospel, the risen Christ appeared to the eleven apostles in Galilee. The Gospel read, "When the disciples saw him, they worshipped, but they doubted." The men chosen by Jesus to build the Church doubted. However, it is important to note that *while* experiencing doubt, they continued to worship.

Permission to doubt has been granted to us. However, the call to worship remains. We worship not in spite of our doubt but in harmony with it. In doing so, we *embrace* the mystery.

The second Trinity nugget actually comes from the glossary of the *Catechism of the Catholic Church*. It reads, "The Trinity is the mystery of three persons: Father, Son, and Holy Spirit. The mystery of the Trinity is inaccessible to the human mind. The revealed truth of the Holy Trinity is at the very root of the Church's living faith as expressed in the Creed."

The Creed, our profession of faith that we'll pray together in a few minutes, states very clearly what we believe as a Church. Don't mechanically mouth the words to this prayer. Rather, focus on what it is saying we believe. *Pray* the words. *Profess* the words.

Simply put, according to the Creed, we have *two* beliefs. We believe in the Trinity, and we believe in the Church.

The Trinity: "I believe in one God—the Father almighty, maker of heaven and earth…Jesus Christ, the Only Begotten Son of God… the Holy Spirit, who proceeds from the Father and the Son."

And the Church: "I believe in one, holy, catholic, and apostolic Church."

We profess to believe in the Trinity and in the Church.

Finally, and I don't remember the source of this third nugget, I offer this image of Trinity: "The Trinity is our creator (God the Father), our human example (Jesus Christ), and our voice (the Holy Spirit)—one God, three gifts." I think that is a beautiful expression of Trinity. It allows me to embrace the mystery.

The Trinity is the *revealed truth* of our faith. Mystery is the *essence* of our faith. After all, isn't faith a belief in something we cannot fully understand? Something we cannot explain or prove?

When we make the sign of the cross, we say, "In the *name* of the Father, and the Son, and the Holy Spirit." Notice we use the singular form "name" rather than the plural "names." One God, three persons.

Each time we make the sign of the cross, we allow the love of the Trinity to dwell in our hearts. We heard in our first reading from Deuteronomy: "Fix in your heart, that the Lord is God…and that there is no other."

Fix the truth and love of the Trinity in your heart. Embrace the mystery.

May 2018

Germination Is Still Possible

Eleventh Sunday in Ordinary Time

Ezekiel 17:22–24
2 Corinthians 5:6–10
Mark 4:26–34

I have the privilege this year of preaching on both Mother's Day *and* Father's Day weekend. Happy Father's Day to all the dads out there!

If you were here on Mother's Day, you might remember that I gave a brief tribute to my wife, and all mothers, by sharing some of the heartfelt and valuable advice Carol had given our children as they grew up. I asked the kids via email to supply me with some of the wisdom she had offered them over the years. They responded with beautiful examples such as "The best advice I ever got from mom was that everyone has a story to tell, and one of the best things we can do is *listen* to their story."

I remember looking out at the congregation as I spoke. People were overwhelmed with emotion hearing the life-changing words of a mother to her children. I also remember your confused looks as you thought, "That Carol is amazing. How did she end up with him?"

Putting humility aside, I thought it would be appropriate to ask my children the same question about me. So I sent the four of them another email, this time asking what advice *I* had given them over the years.

I hit "send" on the email and waited for their responses…and waited. When I sent the email about Carol, all four kids responded within the hour. Two *days* after sending the email about me, I received two responses. Each of the responses began the same way: "I remember some advice that you gave me, but I didn't really follow it."

My eldest daughter said, "You told me to stop trying to fix people." She went on to get a PhD in psychology and now spends her entire professional career trying to fix people.

My youngest son said, "You told me to stop spending so much time in front of the computer." He is now a software engineer and spends his entire professional career in front of a computer.

Both of their responses *ended* the same way as well, each saying, "But I'm sure you meant well when you said it."

We have readings that tie in beautifully with Father's Day. From Ezekiel, we heard, "It shall put forth branches and bear fruit, and become a majestic cedar. Birds of every kind shall dwell beneath it."

From the Gospel of Mark, we heard, "It is like a mustard seed that, when it is sown in the ground, is the smallest of all the seeds on the earth. But once it is sown, it springs up and becomes the largest of plants and puts forth large branches, so that the birds of the sky can dwell in its shade."

Two powerful visual images of a father—the majestic cedar and the large mustard tree, each supplying ample shade and a safe dwelling place in its branches, bearing fruit and planting seeds of wisdom of his own to continue the cycle of life. The confident and proud father, certain of his purpose and direction, or so we'd like to believe.

While this is a powerful image of a father, or of parents in general, the reality is that most of the time, we are just doing what we can and hoping for the best—giving advice and planting seeds we *hope* will produce fruit. As St. Paul wrote in his second letter to the Corinthians, "We walk by faith."

We *must* walk by faith, as the germination rates for our seeds are not that promising.

Agriculturally speaking, the chances of a seed germinating once it has been planted ranges between 40–80 percent and depends on a number of variables.

Likewise, parents learn that a certain percentage of our words of wisdom won't stick. Some advice we offer may not be received or—like my kids—may be ignored altogether.

The same can be said about planting seeds of faith. We do our very best to plant the seeds of faith in those we care about, not only our children but also our family, friends, or those we see as lost and searching for purpose.

We plant the seeds of faith by being intentional disciples—spreading the gospel message, sharing our beliefs and values openly, loving God and others, and acting as feet-washing servants. Even then, we don't know if or when we will see results.

I am not a farmer by trade, but I know enough about planting seeds to know there are things we can do to make germination more likely and increase our chances of bearing fruit.

First, we must use a high-quality seed. Our seeds of faith must be authentic. The soil in which we are planting will be more receptive if the message is genuine. When we sow seeds of faith for show or for personal gain, they will likely fall on rocky soil.

Second, we need to sow the seeds under the right conditions. We must plant the seeds of faith *with* love and *out of* love.

Third, we need persistence. Why not play the odds? If germination rates are only 40–80 percent, why not increase our odds by sowing the seeds of faith more often? Yield will increase with the number of seeds planted.

Fourth, we need patience. Germination will not likely occur overnight or perhaps even for years.

In researching the germination of seeds, I came across the word *quiescence*. Seeds are living organisms. Although a seed may *appear* to be dead, it is actually in a state of quiescence.

Quiescence means that the seed is at rest until desirable conditions trigger germination; the point is, the seed of faith we planted is still alive.

That should provide some level of comfort to those of us who are praying for loved ones who have lost their way on their faith journey. We have planted the seeds. We must be patient—those seeds may not be dead but rather in a state of quiescence. Germination is still possible.

If we use high-quality seeds and sow them with love, and we are persistent and patient, then all there is left to do is walk by faith, trusting that those seeds will germinate.

And when they do germinate, the possibilities are limitless. Remember the mustard seed from today's gospel—the smallest of all the seeds on the earth that becomes the largest of plants after germination.

Planting seeds is an act of faith.

The following is a quote from Henry David Thoreau's work, *Faith in a Seed:* "Though I do not believe a plant will spring up where no seed has been, I have great faith in a seed. Convince me that you have a seed there, and I am prepared to expect wonders."

Please continue to plant the seeds of faith.

June 2018

Jesus Doesn't Love Us All the Same

Thirteenth Sunday of Ordinary Time   Wisdom 1:13–15, 2:23–24
2 Corinthians 8:7, 9, 13–15
Mark 5:21–43

Those who have children insist they play no favorites. In declaring this, they often say, "I love all my kids the same." It may be a matter of semantics, but what they *really* mean to say is that they love them all equally. We can't love them the same because *they* are not the same.

As a dad, I had to learn this by trial and error, but eventually, I learned that while I love my children equally, I *cannot* love them the same. In fact, if I had *tried* to love them the same, I would have failed miserably.

I will use a simple example to make my point. Each of my children handled challenging situations differently; therefore, they needed to be loved and comforted, sometimes healed, differently.

Mary was a thinker. I loved her by talking through tough situations with her, brainstorming ideas and coming up with the best solution.

Rick was a reactor. He often acted impulsively without putting much thought to the big picture. I loved him by being there for him *after* the fact—to catch him if he fell and affirm him if he succeeded.

Laura was all emotions. I loved her by hugging her through whatever the difficult situation was.

Robby was all about time and space. I loved him by giving him both, occasionally letting him know I was available if needed.

I love my kids equally, but I don't love them the same.

This differentiated love came to mind as I read Mark's gospel.

We are introduced to two people in today's "miracle within a miracle" gospel story—Jairus and the hemorrhaging woman.

Jairus was identified by name while the woman remained nameless, indicating she was insignificant. She was an outcast with *no* status in her community. She was, at best, on the fringe of society. We know she was poor; the gospel tells us she was afflicted for twelve years and "spent all she had" on doctors.

Jairus, on the other hand, was a synagogue official—a position of honor, wealth, power, and influence.

Both the woman and Jairus conveyed a sense of urgency. Each was literally dealing with a life-or-death situation—the woman with her own fragile health and Jairus with a daughter near death.

On its surface, the story is about a strong faith being rewarded. However, it is clear that the actions of both the woman and Jairus were prompted by *desperation* rather than by a strong faith.

Neither was a disciple of Jesus, nor did they hang on his every word or help spread his message. They didn't *know* Jesus; they only knew *of* him. To take it a step further, as a synagogue official Jairus spoke out *against* Jesus and his message.

My point is that the woman and Jairus were *not* faith-filled followers intuitively turning to Jesus in their time of need.

They were desperate people who were willing to do *anything* or approach *anyone* who could possibly help their situation.

The hemorrhaging woman had tried doctor after doctor while suffering for twelve years. She had heard about this Jesus person and the rumors of miracles and healing. When word came that he would be traveling through town, what did she have to lose?

This sickly woman knew she would never get past the crowd for a face-to-face encounter, so she did what she could. She reached through the crowd in the hope of touching his clothing.

Her actions came out of desperation rather than faith.

Faith came later when she realized it had *worked*. Her act of faith came when she dropped to her knees. The gospel says, "She fell down before Jesus and told him the whole truth."

I believe the "whole truth" included an honest account of her *lack* of faith over the years and admitting that it was desperation that led her to reach out and touch his clothing. The whole truth included confirmation that her encounter with Jesus had changed her life forever.

In the gospel account, Jesus said, "Your faith has saved you."

I was not there at the time, but I believe what Jesus meant was, "This first step toward faith has saved you."

Jairus, too, acted out of desperation. Wealth put all medical resources at his disposal—to no avail. His money, power, and influence provided no help. His years of studying Jewish law and earning the respect of the community were of no use—his daughter was dying.

So he set aside his public anti-Jesus stance. Desperate times called for desperate measures.

Jairus *humbled* himself by dropping to his knees and asking for Jesus's help. Anyone who knew him or was aware of his position as a synagogue official would have been stunned by his actions. He threw his career out the window in this act of desperation—not act of *faith* but an act of desperation.

Jairus's act of faith came later. When he was notified that his daughter had died, Jesus told him, "Do not be afraid; just have faith."

Again, I was not there, but I think what Jesus meant was, "Do not be afraid. Just take this first step toward faith."

Jairus took that first step toward faith when, despite being told his daughter was dead, he led Jesus into his home to lay his hands on her.

Jesus loved and healed the woman, responding to her act of desperation and leading her to faith. Jesus loved Jairus and healed his daughter, responding to his act of desperation and leading him to faith. Jesus loved all who came to him equally—not the same, but equally.

His love continues. He loves those who come to him with unwavering faith as well as those who approach cautiously with unanswered questions and lingering doubt. He loves those whose faith is intermittent, a cycle of belief and doubt and unbelief. And as we heard today, He loves those who turn to Him in desperation.

Jesus loves us all equally. He loves and heals us as we need to be loved and healed.

July 2018

One More

Seventeenth Sunday in Ordinary Time   2 Kings 4:42–44
                                       Ephesians 4:1–6
                                       John 6:1–15

I just returned from a quick trip to New Orleans. I attended a conference for deacons that was celebrating the fifty-year anniversary of the restoration of the permanent diaconate. It was a great event, with daily Mass celebrated by priests and bishops from around the country.

On the first day, Cardinal Tobin was the main celebrant. He began his homily by sharing this story: He was recessing out the main aisle of the cathedral following Mass, blessing the people as he walked. Near the back, a young girl was standing partially out in the aisle. She had her hands on her hips. The look on her face he described as "somewhere between curiosity and disgust." When he got near her, he stopped and looked down.

She said, "I have a question."

He squatted down in front of her and said, "Of course. What's your question?"

She asked, again with disgust, "Why can't you take off your own hat?"

He said he was struck by her sincerity and amused by her approach. However, he also came to a realization at that moment. He didn't know the answer!

He smiled at the little girl and said, "I'm not sure, sweetheart. Maybe it's a union thing."

He used the story to emphasize that sometimes in life, particularly a life of ministry, we are asked questions we can't answer. One of those questions, a recurring one, is, "What does God expect of me?"

In last week's gospel, Jesus encouraged His disciples: "Come away by yourselves to a deserted place and rest awhile."

Fr. Jim's homily emphasized the need for us to take time to step away and renew ourselves. We need to stay strong for the work that lies ahead.

In today's gospel, we find out why Jesus emphasized the importance of rest and renewal. There was much to do. Many people were in need. Many people needed to be fed, both literally and figuratively.

In this gospel story, we heard about the feeding of the five thousand. In John's version, Jesus asked Philip, "Where can we buy enough food for them to eat?"

And there it is, as Cardinal Tobin referenced, the question that cannot be answered. It is the question that leads us to wonder, "What is it that God expects of me?"

The gospel goes on to say that Jesus said this to test Philip. He threw down the gauntlet: "There are many hungry people. What are you going to do about it?"

Philip's response reflects the overwhelming enormity of the situation. He said, "Two hundred days' wages worth of food would not be enough for each of them to have even a little."

What Philip was saying, and he spoke for all the disciples, was, "What you are asking of us is impossible!"

It was a question that could not be answered. If it was a test, Philip failed. In his defense, placed in the same situation, most of us would have failed as well. According to Philip, what Jesus asked of him was too much; it was impossible.

What was the right answer? What answer was Jesus expecting Philip to give? Hoping he would give? Perhaps something like this: "I will do what I can to feed as many as I can, and I will encourage the other disciples to do the same."

As Christians, we are faced with this dilemma daily. There are so many people in need, and Jesus is asking us the tough question: "What are you going to do about it?"

It is more than challenging; it is overwhelming.

Carol and I recently went on vacation, our "come away and rest" time. Upon returning, we made the mistake of writing up a lengthy "to-do" list of all we needed to accomplish for our various ministries, not to mention our family. Afterward, Carol sat down next to me and sighed. "Let's just get back on the plane. There's no way we can get all this done."

I'm sure you have all experienced that feeling at some point, wanting to escape from what Jesus is asking of you.

Perhaps you spend your days as a caregiver, providing round-the-clock care for a spouse or other family member. That "come away and rest" time may only be a few minutes of prayer before bed or a brief respite when your loved one dozes off unexpectedly.

You're a parent—one child has the flu and is getting sick on the sheets you just changed; another needs help with math homework that you don't understand; and a third needs a ride to soccer practice, and he can't find his shoes. You're overwhelmed.

You might be involved in any number of other ministries:

- Volunteering at a soup kitchen and seeing the endless line of people who are hungry, entire families in need.
- Serving the homeless on the streets and noticing there are more people this week than there were last week. You experience their great need and feel their hopelessness.
- Ministering to people with addictions. Ten days sober before falling again. One month sober, then a relapse.
- Working as a teacher—so many kids with so many needs; and you're expected to teach them, counsel them, affirm them, love them and keep them safe.

It's all overwhelming, so you consider telling Jesus, "I can't do this anymore!" Warning: If you say this, He will lock eyes with you and lovingly say, "Feed my sheep."

That is what God expects from us. He expects us to see the needs of others through the eyes of our faith.

There was a movie based on a true story and released in 2016 titled *Hacksaw Ridge*. While it may not be for everyone because of its graphic depictions of war, it is a powerful movie with a beautiful message.

Private Desmond Doss was a medic and walked into one of the bloodiest battles of World War II without a weapon, armed only with his med kit, his Bible, and his faith in God.

The battle took place in April 1945. The battlefield, known as Hacksaw Ridge, was located on top of a sheer four-hundred-foot cliff. Once US troops engaged with the Japanese on that spot, the mission to take control of the area was deemed untenable, and Doss's decimated battalion was ordered to retreat.

However, Doss refused to leave his injured comrades behind. Facing heavy artillery fire, Doss repeatedly ran back into the kill zone alone, carried wounded soldiers, including some Japanese soldiers, to the edge of the cliff, and singlehandedly lowered them down to safety with a rope. He was absolutely exhausted, and his hands were bloodied and raw from the rope. Each time he saved a man's life, Doss prayed aloud, "Lord, please help me get *one more*."

By the end of the night, he had rescued an estimated seventy-five men.

That is what God expects of us. He wants *that* to be our response to the great need in our world.

The easy road when we are overwhelmed is to leave the work to others. Instead, we must put our trust in Jesus and pray, "Lord, please help me serve one more."

July 2018

Wherever We Need Him to Be

Twentieth Sunday of Ordinary Time   Revelation 11:19; 12:1–6, 10
Ephesians 5:15–20
John 6:51–58

A few years back, multiple teen suicides occurred in central Indiana within a very short period of time. The loss of young lives gave us pause, particularly those of us involved in ministry to young people. The incidents were particularly difficult for high school students grappling with their own identities and self-doubts.

It led to questions: Why is this happening? Who is next? Will our school be affected? And a common question in times of unfathomable loss or grief or tragedy—where is God in all this?

After the first suicide, we came together as a school to pray for the repose of the young man's soul and for peace and comfort for his family and friends. Later, after the third suicide in a month, I remember bringing our school community together again. Everyone—students, faculty, support staff, and administration. We came together again to pray, but we also gathered to ask the question aloud that so many of us had stuck in our heads: "Where *is* God in this?"

I knew I needed to respond to that question for our students, but until I opened my mouth, I had no idea what that response would be. This is what I shared with them:

> Where is God in this? First, know that God cries right along with us when a young person takes his own life. He grieves and mourns with us. A

young person taking his own life is not part of His plan, and so He mourns.

Where is God in this? He is wherever we need him to be. If we need to be angry at Him—He is there; we can let Him have it. If we need comfort, He will wrap His loving arms around us. If we just need to talk, no one is a better listener. If we need to sit in silence and reflect, we can be assured that He is sitting right beside us.

Where is He right now? Right here. When we gather together like this, we are the Body of Christ. We are Him.

So why do I share these words with you now? Because the Church is mired in scandal—unbelievable acts of abuse committed by clergy are coming to light day after day; evil is being exposed.

Of course, we are deeply saddened and pray for the victims of the abuse. We denounce the abusers and cry out for justice…and demand a purification of the Church. All the while that same nagging question echoes in our heads, "Why? Where is God in this?"

I believe the same response I shared with our students rings true in this situation: God cries along with us. This was not part of His plan; this was not His will. He suffers alongside us in the midst of our brokenness. *God is wherever we need Him to be.*

If we need to be angry at Him, we can vent. If we need comfort, He will provide it. If we just need to talk, He is sitting right beside us.

With today's gospel, we conclude chapter 6 of John—known as the Bread of Life Discourse. For the last several weeks, we have heard this message repeatedly: I am the bread of life. I am the living bread come down from heaven. Eat of this bread, and you shall live forever.

Chapter 6 of John is the foundation, the core of our faith. The Eucharist is the source and summit of our faith.

Where is God in all this? He is right there (gesturing to the altar). He is right there where He has always been. Sacrificing Himself on the altar for us.

In these troubling times, some will reject Christ and His Church. Others will go about seeking God elsewhere. How could He possibly exist in this corrupt and abusive Church? He *must* be somewhere else.

The Church is *not* the abusive clergy, *or* the criminal use of power, *or* the look-the-other-way mentality.

The *Church* is the sacrifice that takes place on this altar. The *Church* is those of us who gather in communion to pray together and to be fed, to be nourished by this bread of life. The Church is not merely a building or an institution.

This *altar* is the Church. *We* are the Church—a living, breathing, life-giving being.

If we want change to occur, we must be that change. Our presence here, our participation in the Eucharist, is critical. All of us have been invited to the celebratory banquet.

We heard it in our readings today. In Proverbs, "She has spread her table…come, eat of my food, and drink of the wine."

In John's gospel, "I am the living bread that came down from heaven; *whoever* eats this bread will live forever."

We must RSVP to the invitation. We must answer the call. The Eucharist equips us for daily life and for eternal life. *True food. True drink.* We can't offer to others what we don't take in ourselves.

And that is the true meaning of Church, isn't it? Taking it out to others? As intentional disciples that is our charge.

Pope Francis recently told a group of young people struggling with what is happening in the Church: "We fight scandal by giving witness to the gospel."

In reading through some of the responses to all that is going on in the Church, one priest reflected: "As a priest, I'm not ignoring the horror and tragedy of McCarrick or the reports of past abuse in Pennsylvania. I'm focusing on the souls in front of me, on the Grace of the Sacraments, and on the power of Christ to purify us all. Because I don't really know what else to do or say."

Perhaps St. Paul gives us the best advice in his letter to the Ephesians we heard today: "Watch carefully how you live…making the most of the opportunity…play to the Lord in your hearts, giving thanks always and for everything."

That is what we, the Body of Christ, are called to do. Do it, and God will be with you. He will be wherever you need Him to be.

August 2018

View from the Corner Office

Twenty-fifth Sunday in Ordinary Time

Wisdom 2:17–20
James 3:16–4:3
Mark 9:30–37

I want to begin by talking about the corner office. In the many lavish office buildings that dot the skyline, the corner offices are the most desirable offices on each floor. The corner office is usually larger and has windows on two sides. There is an assumed prestige that comes with occupying a corner office. If you have met Fr. Jim in his office, you may have noticed that it is a corner office, well-suited to his status as our pastor. If you looked for my office, you would discover I don't have one—well-suited to my status as deacon.

In addition, the higher the floor, the more prestige the occupant enjoys. The goal for many who work hard each day is to eventually make it to the corner office of the top floor. Those who do have "made it" in the business world.

We want to be the best, or be perceived as the best, and that top floor corner office is evidence.

Titles may also afford one honor and prestige: regional manager, district supervisor, chairman of the board, chief executive officer, etc.

If we are honest with ourselves, many of us covet that corner office and that prestigious title. We are a little jealous that our work space is smaller and darker and that our job does not come with a fancy title.

I have to confess that I have fallen prey to this myself.

I remember being interviewed once while serving as director of Fatima Retreat House. When the interviewer was done, she said she wanted to verify a few things for her story. She asked me to spell my last name and then asked for my official title. When I said I was the director, she said, "*Just* director? Or executive director?"

You would not believe how close I came to saying, "Executive director." The way she'd said it made it sound very important. I replied sadly, "Just director."

Many of you know I was recently named the director of the Permanent Deacon Formation program for Saint Meinrad. This appointment ushered in a brief battle with humility. When I moved into my big new office, I sent a text to Carol. I could have written something like "I am humbled by this appointment. The cemetery of the Benedictine monks is visible from my window. To be on this holy ground with these men of prayer is an honor."

Wouldn't that have been a beautiful text?

However, that is not what my text said. Instead, my text was accompanied by two pictures—one of the interior of my office and another of my name and title on the door. The words of my text read, "Check this out! I'm a pretty big deal down here!"

Today's readings speak to the downside of this way of thinking, beginning with the words we heard in the Letter from James: "Where jealousy and selfish ambition exist, there is disorder."

Jesus called his apostles to task when he discovered they were engaged in their own "corner office discussions." The gospel says they were "*discussing among themselves who was the greatest.*"

The apostles were already in corner offices. From among all the disciples, they had been chosen. They held the title of *apostle*; they were a part of *The Twelve* and recognized as the favored disciples.

Even so, that was not enough. Individually, each wanted to be recognized as the *greatest* of the twelve. A corner office was not enough; they wanted the corner office on the top floor.

Jesus used it as a teaching moment. "If anyone wishes to be first," Jesus said, "he shall be the last of all and the servant of all." I am sure his words embarrassed and humbled the apostles.

With these simple words, He imparted a powerful message. You were not chosen in order to be honored; you were chosen to serve others. The title of apostle is not one of prestige but one of servitude.

You do not do my work for personal gain but rather for the glory of God.

So what did Jesus mean by *the servant of all?* Being the servant of all was more than healing, comforting, and otherwise meeting the needs of the people that approached them. It was more than teaching on a hillside or preaching in the temple. It was even more than miraculously feeding five thousand people with a few loaves and some fish.

Truly being the servant of all meant *seeking out* those most in need, looking beyond the crowds to the fringes of society. It meant touching the leper. It meant conversing with beggars. It meant entering the homes of widows and visiting prisoners. Being the servant of all meant being a voice for the voiceless and serving others who could offer nothing in return. When you are the servant of all, there is no immediate payback or recognition, and you will not earn a corner office.

Jesus wanted to emphasize what he meant by *servant of all* by placing a small child in their midst. Children are bundles of need, completely helpless. They need to be fed, clothed, sheltered, and protected. And of course, they need unconditional love, the love that can only come from a servant's heart.

When we help those who cannot help themselves, as a parent loves a child, we reveal a servant's heart.

Who is the child whom Jesus has put in *our* midst, the helpless person in need of the unconditional love of a servant's heart?

Is it a spouse or loved one with failing health? Who needs around-the-clock care...needs fed, bathed, and dressed?

Is it the young father at the soup kitchen who *wants* to provide for his family and simply cannot? Or the single mother at the shelter who has nowhere else to go?

Is it the isolated person suffering from depression? The one who needs someone with a servant's heart to tell him he has value? That he is loved?

Is it the completely helpless unborn child whose mother is contemplating abortion? A child who needs someone to be his voice?

Or maybe the helpless child is someone who is *always* in our midst—a spouse, parent, or child who is *temporarily* helpless while going through a difficult time. Can we be selfless enough to turn our attention toward that person in his or her time of need?

What about the friends or coworkers who currently feel helpless as they struggle with what is going on in our Church? Can we lend them an ear? Encourage them? The problems of the Church will not be resolved from the top down but from the inside out. Can we be selfless enough to facilitate that inside healing for those who feel helpless?

Referring to the completely dependent child in their midst, Jesus told his apostles, "Whoever receives *one* child such as this in my name, receives me."

That is our payback. There is no earthly payback, but the view from heaven is far more beautiful than the view from *any* corner office.

September 2018

Don't Hoard the Work of God

Twenty-sixth Sunday in Ordinary Time   Numbers 11:25–29
                                        James 5:1–6
                                        Mark 9:38–43, 45, 47–48

Today's readings make a strong argument for Christian unity.

Allow me to share a couple of stories, then we'll connect the dots.

Last spring, I reached out to the class of 2019 to encourage them to sign up to be mentors for our incoming freshmen class. Each freshman is assigned to a senior mentor. Those seniors help the new freshmen navigate the transition to high school and provide them with an experienced person to meet with regularly.

As the deadline approached, the number of students who had signed up to be a mentor was low, and I became concerned that we would not have enough.

I wondered if I should open up the opportunity to be a mentor to the junior class to help fill the gap. I contacted the seniors and offered two options for their consideration. Option one, expand our mentor pool by including juniors. Option two, each of the seniors who had signed up would take on two or three additional freshmen.

Their response was swift and overwhelming—*no juniors*. They told me in no uncertain terms, "Mentoring is for seniors." They would rather take on more work for themselves than include juniors in the mentor program.

As it turned out, a few more seniors signed up, so it became a nonissue. However, I found their solidarity in excluding juniors from the program very interesting.

I attended the Right to Life dinner earlier this week. It was a good-sized crowd of approximately nine hundred people. I was in the midst of uncomfortable small talk with someone I'd just met when she gestured to the crowd and said, "It's nice to see nine hundred Catholics come together for such a great cause."

When it comes to small talk, I am usually looking for the quickest way out, so normally, I would just agree and move on. But there was something in the way she said it that compelled me to respond. "It's a great cause for people of any faith," I replied.

She looked at me with a blank stare. "Well," I said, "not everyone here is Catholic."

Now she was the one looking for a quick way out. She nodded at me and walked away. I got the distinct impression that I had somehow offended her.

Was she offended because I hadn't simply agreed with her? Or was she offended because she thought prolife somehow belonged to Catholics? Did she think prolife was "ours"?

Oftentimes, our Sunday readings will follow a pattern: The Old Testament selection and the gospel will mirror one another while the second reading offers an exclamation point on the message. We have such a set of readings today.

The first reading from the Book of Numbers and the Gospel of Mark tell virtually the same story: There were people out there preaching or healing without permission—people acting for the greater good but without the expressed authority to do so. In both stories, those who did have permission or authority were bothered. They went to Moses, or Jesus depending on the story, and reported these rebels. They not only turned them in, but they also told Moses and Jesus exactly how to handle the situation.

Allow me to take a few liberties here as I paraphrase the stories.

A summary of our first reading: "Moses, there are two men out there spreading God's word. They weren't with us when we all received the spirit, so they should not be allowed to spread God's word. Only we get to do that. Moses, you must stop them!"

To which Moses replied, "Stop them? I wish everyone would spread God's word!"

And summarizing the Gospel, "Jesus, we saw someone driving out demons in your name. He is not one of us—only we are allowed to drive out demons in your name. You need to stop him!"

To which Jesus replied, "Stop him? I wish everyone would drive out demons in my name!"

To help with our understanding, there are two questions to consider.

Question 1: "Why did those who complained get so upset by what they saw?"

It's a simple matter of fairness. Those two men were not present when the spirit came upon the group, so it's not fair that they were allowed to spread God's word just like the others.

That man driving out demons in the name of Jesus is not even a disciple. It is not fair that he got to drive out demons just like the disciples.

Question 2: "Why were Moses and Jesus not bothered by the behaviors that were reported to them?"

Simply put, Moses and Jesus were results-oriented. Should they be concerned with who is spreading God's word and driving out demons and whether or not they had the authority to do so? Should they limit the number of people doing God's work? *Or* should they be grateful to anyone who is willing to help?

It boils down to perspective. The perspective of those that complained was egocentric. They sought to limit the work of God to a select few, a group to which they belonged. God's work was their domain, just as mentoring is only for seniors and prolife support is only for Catholics.

The complainers wanted to hoard God's work, and the grace that comes with it, for themselves. James described this phenomenon in today's second reading: "You have stored up treasure for the last days...you have fattened your hearts." That is the exclamation point I mentioned earlier: Don't hoard the work of God!

By comparison, the perspective of Moses and Jesus focused on the greater good. When it comes to doing God's work here on earth, there is no such thing as too many laborers. If you are filled with the spirit as you spread God's word, you are welcome on our team. If you drive out demons in the name of the Lord, you are welcome on our team.

The Catholic Church differs from other Christian denominations in some of its fundamental beliefs. However, we have many more commonalities with other Christians than we have differences.

When it comes to addressing the general welfare of the people of God—such as spreading the gospel message, caring for the poor, and loving our neighbor—the more, the merrier.

We should rejoice in our Catholic faith and embrace its rich teachings and traditions. We should also rejoice in the fact that we are not expected to do God's work alone; all Christians are called to share in the load. More work gets done when no one cares who gets the credit.

We do His work not to earn points or gain special graces but for the greater good of the Body of Christ.

Don't hoard the work of God!

September 2018

Path to Holiness

Twenty-Ninth Sunday in Ordinary Time

Isaiah 53:10–11

Hebrews 4:14–16

Mark 10:35–45

When I need advice or help with a particular problem, I tend to go to someone with expertise in that area or someone who has experienced the same situation. Whether they succeeded or failed, at least they have been through it and can share their experience.

It's why I used to call my dad when I had car trouble. It's why our kids came to us when it was time to potty-train their own kids. It's why our parish has married couples facilitate marriage preparation for engaged couples. We share with them the highs and lows of marriage, along with the pitfalls to avoid.

We want to be sure our mentor has real-life expertise. For instance, I want to learn to drive a car from someone who has driven before, not someone who has only read about driving. When I hire someone, I don't depend on a paper resume alone; I make some phone calls to people who have worked with the applicant to get real-life input.

This desire for practical expertise comes to mind for two reasons: the recent canonization of seven individuals to sainthood and today's reading from the letter to the Hebrews.

I was inspired by the canonizations. They were signs of hope and encouragement in an age when both are lacking. These men and women, now saints, were ordinary people who accomplished extraordinary things. These ordinary people were sinners like us who stumbled and fell while on their journey, eventually finding solid footing and continuing their pursuit of goodness, truth, beauty, justice, and love.

My wife Carol attended the canonizations. The priest who traveled with the group emphasized that they were there as *pilgrims*, not tourists. This concept resonated with me. Tourists are looking around, taking in the sights. But pilgrims are searching, in this case, searching for the path that would lead them closer to Jesus.

I believe many of us are tourists. We like the sights and sounds of our faith and want to take them all in. However, when it comes to the searching, digging deeper for meaning and understanding or grabbing hold of opportunities to grow closer to Jesus, we are hesitant.

Perhaps it is doubt that is holding us back. We don't feel worthy; we're not holy enough. Why bother searching for something that is out of our reach? I recently read Matthew Kelly's new book titled *The Biggest Lie in the History of Christianity*. Spoiler alert: Kelly states that the biggest lie is that we, the ordinary believer, cannot achieve holiness.

Which brings me back to the seven individuals who were canonized as saints last Sunday and the hope and encouragement I mentioned. They are real-life proof that holiness *is* possible. They have practical experience from which we can learn.

As a child, the man who would eventually become St. Pope Paul VI was sickly and would often not be able to go to school due to bouts of illness. Before pursuing priesthood, he was a lawyer and dabbled in journalism. He was an ordinary man, a tourist, experiencing life. He was not born holier than us; he eventually sought holiness by becoming a pilgrim.

The man canonized as St. Oscar Romero was born into a family of ten in El Salvador. Their home had no electricity or running water. He only went to traditional school until the age of twelve. He worked as an apprentice carpenter and helped his dad as a postal carrier until entering seminary. While in seminary, he needed to leave for an extended time to support the family when his mother became ill. Oscar Romero experienced life—real-life challenges and sorrows.

He was not born a saint; he *became* a saint. He was assassinated as he celebrated Mass. That doesn't happen to tourists.

St. Sr. Nazaria Mesa was born in Madrid, Spain, and was one of eighteen children. Growing up, her family was indifferent and sometimes even hostile to her desire to enter religious life. However, she was a pilgrim and later led several family members back to the Church.

New saint, Maria Kasper, attended very little school because of poor health. Despite this, she began to help the poor, the abandoned, and the sick at a young age. After her father died when she was twenty-one, she worked the land as a farm hand for about ten cents a day. Her helpfulness toward others attracted other women to her, and she felt a call to the religious life. Later, she and four other women officially took vows of poverty, chastity, and obedience and formed the Poor Handmaids of Jesus Christ. Maria was ordinary. *Saint* Maria was extraordinary.

The other three new saints have very similar stories. Despite hardships and challenges, these seven new saints made the decision to be pilgrims. Being a tourist was not enough for them. They were *seekers*. As pilgrims, they lived the message of the gospel: *Seek and you will find.*

We are all called to sainthood, to transition from tourist to pilgrim. Holiness *is* possible.

In our second reading from the letter to the Hebrews we heard, "For we do not have a high priest who is unable to sympathize with our weaknesses, but one who has similarly been tested in every way… So let us confidently approach the throne…to find grace."

This passage reminds us that we can confidently turn to Jesus. He had real-life experience. He understands what we are going through and can help us. He was fully human and experienced all the temptation and evil that the world threw at Him, just like us. His humanity shows us that it is possible to live a holy life. It is not without its challenges; in fact, it is extremely difficult—but it *is* possible.

Just as we turn to a mechanic for help with our car, we look to the saints and turn to Christ for their expertise. We do this for real-life examples of holiness and the realization that holiness is possible.

Being a tourist has its advantages. It is much simpler. We can pick and choose what we see and do. We look around and take in the sights and sounds of the world. However, when it comes to our faith, we are called to be pilgrims. Admittedly, it is more challenging. We must have purpose and be willing to do the work—to search for understanding and meaning.

Tourists appreciate the beauty of the Church. Pilgrims *are* the beauty of the Church.

The path of the tourist leads us back home. The path of the pilgrim leads us to holiness.

October 2018

Begin with Heaven in Mind

Thirty-third Sunday in Ordinary Time   Daniel 12:1–3
Hebrews 10:11–4; 18
Mark 13:24–32

Fr. Eugene Hensell is a long-time instructor at Saint Meinrad, teaching Scripture courses to seminarians. He is known to have regular pop quizzes on material from prior lectures, emphasizing the importance of ongoing preparation for the ultimate goal of passing the final exam at the end of the course.

Years ago, on the Monday after Thanksgiving, a seminarian made the mistake of assuming Fr. Eugene would not give a pop quiz the first day after Thanksgiving break.

Much to his dismay, there *was* a pop quiz. Knowing he was totally unprepared, he wrote at the top of the paper, "Jesus, Mary, and Joseph…Save me!"

He failed the quiz miserably. Under the seminarian's "Save me!" note, Fr. Eugene drew a picture of a drowning man and wrote, "Too late!"

Archbishop Thompson celebrated Mass here last night and shared that story. It fit in well with my homily, so I borrowed it to use today.

Message: You must prepare if you want to reach your goal.

Many of you are likely familiar with the *Leader in Me* program here at St. Pius X School. The framework is based on Stephen Covey's *Seven Habits of Highly Effective People* and works to instill these same types of work habits in the students, such as being proactive and putting first things first.

Number 2 on the list of habits is to *begin with the end in mind*.

The idea is that we begin by establishing our goal first. What is it that we want to accomplish? Then, with that goal in mind, we determine what must happen in order for us to attain that goal. We start with the goal and work backward. Ultimately, we get to step #1, our starting point. With both step #1 and our end goal established, our plan is in place.

As for me, I try to be highly effective. Sometimes I am, and sometimes I'm not. Sometimes I plan, and sometimes I wing it. However, I am not haphazard. The more important something is to me, the more likely I am to begin with the end in mind. When something is *truly* important, I devise a plan.

Is reaching heaven important to you? You need a plan; begin with heaven in mind.

Today is the final Sunday in ordinary time. Next Sunday, we will celebrate the Feast of Christ the King before beginning the Advent season. Leading into Advent, the Church will often use "end of the world" scripture to set the table.

In the reading from the Book of the Prophet Daniel, we heard these words: "It shall be a time unsurpassed in distress…Many of those who sleep in the dust of the earth shall awake; some shall live forever, others shall be an everlasting horror and disgrace."

In the Gospel of Mark, Jesus told His disciples: "In those days after that tribulation the sun will be darkened, and the moon will not give its light, and the stars will be falling from the sky, and the powers in the heavens will be shaken."

This message is not the most uplifting and reassuring. Such scripture is often referred to as *apocalyptic*. The word conjures up doom and gloom. However, it is interesting to note that the word *apocalyptic* is of Greek origin, and its root means "unveil." Thinking of the end in those terms is much less unsettling.

When we unveil something, we pull back the cover. We know what is under there; we just don't know exactly what it will look like. We unveil a work of art—we know it is a work of art under that sheet. We may have even seen it in its early stages, but we anticipate seeing the final product.

The Indy 500 pace car is unveiled each year. We know there is a car under that sheet; we anxiously await what kind of car it is.

Today's readings unveil the end of time. We *know* our time on earth will come to an end. We don't know how or when, but it *is* certain.

While this certainly sends the signal that we must be prepared, it should not cause us undue anxiety or stress. After all, we *know* what's under the sheet; we just aren't sure exactly what it will look like.

Mark's gospel and modern thinking stand in conflict.

In today's church, many Christians seem to think, "Since the time of Jesus's coming cannot be known, we don't need to think much about it." Mark draws the opposite conclusion. He claims that since the timing is unknown, we should think about it all the time!

Modern Christians often think, "Since the time is unknown, it could be hundred, or thousands, or millions of years from now." Mark draws a very different conclusion. Since the timing is unknown, it could be today! Maybe this evening, or at midnight, or when dawn breaks.

Mark clearly wants this to be part of the faith that informs our daily lives. If heaven is important to us, we need a plan. If heaven is the end we have in mind, where do we begin?

Whatever first step we decide upon, our faith tells us it should *not* come from a place of fear but rather one of joy. If we act out of fear, we will do so hesitantly, lacking conviction and purpose. Our actions will tend to be self-centered, as we attempt to protect ourselves from the unknown.

However, as Christians, our hope is in the resurrection. We believe this life is but a prelude to eternal life in the kingdom of God. That knowledge should bring us joy. The steps in our plan to reach heaven, in our daily lives, will be carried out joyfully. Those actions will be based upon love of God and others, and we will act with confidence.

The result? A joyful life, not based on fear, will unfold naturally. When we begin with the end in mind, we live a life of purpose.

How important is reaching heaven to you?

November 2018

Some Blisters Are a Good Thing

First Sunday of Advent

Jeremiah 33:14–16
1 Thessalonians 3:12–4:2
Luke 21:25–26

I would like to begin by offering two analogies regarding today's gospel reading.

Analogy #1: I bought a new pair of dress shoes recently. Many adults wear dress shoes every day for work. Most of us don't have the luxury of rolling out of bed each day, putting on colorful socks, and slipping into a pair of sandals—like a certain priest I know. (Note to reader: Our pastor, Fr. Jim Farrell, is famous for wearing sandals along with a pair of liturgically correct colored socks.)

I own a total of *one* pair of dress shoes at a time. I will wear that pair as long as I can, squeezing every bit of life out of them. Once I wear a hole in the soles of the shoes, I will continue to wear them for another six months. Then I buy a pair of cushioned inserts to put in the shoes and wear them for another six months. I am not a penny-pincher. There are just some things I hate to change. My former shoes were comfortable, and it took time and effort to get them to that point.

I dread buying new shoes. I know that no pair will feel as good or as comfortable as my former pair. I'll walk funny for two weeks as I adjust to the new shoes. I'll get blisters. Why must I be uncomfortable?

Analogy #2: When I was younger, I could drive forever without getting tired. Now I start yawning after about twenty minutes.

There is something about traveling in the car; I settle in and get comfortable. The suspension provides a smooth ride. There is climate control temperature, easy-listening music playing, adjustable steering wheel and seat, and cruise control. Everything is just the way I like it. Everything that sold me on the car is now putting me in danger because it makes me sleepy.

With my work at Saint Meinrad requiring regular three-hour trips to southern Indiana, I turned to audiobooks for help.

The books keep me sharp and alert, or as the gospel would say, the books keep me vigilant. My senses are heightened. I am being exposed to something new; I need to pay attention, or I'll miss something. I am *not* sleepy, *and* I arrive refreshed and ready to go.

In preparation for preaching, I make it a habit to read the readings of the day slowly to see what word or phrase jumps out at me. Sometimes, it is a familiar phrase that brings to mind a memory. It might be a word or phrase I've never before seen. And then there are times, as is the case today, when a word or phrase seems out of place or is used in an unusual context.

In Luke's gospel, Jesus warns his disciples, "Beware that your hearts do not become drowsy."

A drowsy heart…

Scripture *often* speaks to the condition of our hearts: a deceitful heart, a pure and upright heart, a cheerful heart, a strong heart, a heart full of wisdom, and many more, but a *drowsy* heart?

Why did Jesus warn his disciples—warn us—not to allow our hearts to become drowsy?

Just like I cling to my old shoes for comfort, our *hearts* can settle for what is comfortable. The way I love God and others is always the way I've loved God and others—nothing more, nothing less. For you, that may mean attending Mass every Sunday, leading a Bible study once per month, and writing an annual check to a deserving charity.

Those are all beautiful expressions of faith, expressions I pray you'll continue. However, Jesus warns us to beware of complacency. Should these faith habits become too mechanical, with no energy or thought behind them, we can slip into cruise control and create a false sense of security—"I'm sure I'll get to heaven. All is well." It is an attitude that can cause our hearts to become drowsy.

A heart becomes drowsy when there is nothing new to nourish it or invigorate it. Thus, Jesus encourages us to "be vigilant at all times."

To be vigilant means keeping careful watch, to be on the lookout for danger, for anything that might get in the way of our ultimate goal of attaining heaven. Vigilance requires awareness not only of enemies and threats from the outside world but also of the weaknesses within us—complacency, overconfidence, and drowsy hearts.

As comfortable as our old shoes are, the time will come when a change is needed. As comfortable as adjusted seats and cruise control may be, we can't allow ourselves to become drowsy—so drowsy that we drive off the road or miss our exit.

Jesus tells us, "Beware that your hearts do not become drowsy" and "be vigilant at all times." He is telling us, as we enter Advent, that we need to get comfortable with being *un*comfortable.

We need the equivalent of audiobooks for our faith. What can we add to our faith routine to keep us sharp and alert or expose us to something new—to keep us vigilant? What will heighten our senses? What can we do to stir our drowsy hearts?

First and foremost, prayer keeps us vigilant. For those that argue, "I don't pray that much—I *live* my faith. I'm a doer."

That's awesome; *do* prayer. Praying is living your faith too.

Prayer is an engaging conversation with God. It stimulates our relationship with Him. It prevents our hearts from becoming drowsy.

We attend Mass—that is certainly a beautiful form of communal prayer. What else can we do this Advent season?

Maybe it is time to dust off our rosaries. Maybe it is time to learn how to pray the liturgy of the hours—there is even an app for that! Maybe it is time to *make* time for Adoration. Or maybe it is as simple as taking ten minutes each day to sit and talk directly to God—share your hopes, dreams, worries, and anxieties.

Prayer keeps us vigilant. It is a great way to prevent a drowsy heart, but it is not the only way: Take advantage of opportunities to go to confession. Consider involving yourself in one of the many ministries of the parish, volunteering, visiting the sick, picking up the phone to console someone who has experienced loss, or providing a listening ear for someone going through a difficult time.

"Beware that your hearts do not become drowsy." We can't allow ourselves to become complacent. Whatever your faith practices are, add something new to the mix.

Sometimes blisters are a good thing. They show that we are active and have made necessary changes in our lives.

December 2018

"If You're Sick of Christmas by December 25th, You Haven't Done Advent Correctly"

Second Sunday of Advent

Baruch 5:1–9
Philippians 1:4–6, 8–11
Luke 3:1–6

I want to talk a bit about traditions—specifically family Christmas traditions. We all have them. We may be embarrassed by some of them because they are a bit odd, but deep down, we are proud of them and wouldn't change them for the world. They may be odd traditions, but they are *our* odd traditions.

Our family is no different. I could talk for days about our family Christmas traditions, but in the interest of time, I will zero in on just two.

First, there are the Christmas Eve "nachos." I use air quotes as I say nachos because to call them nachos is an affront to authentic Mexican restaurants everywhere. If you promise to keep this between us, I'll share the recipe:

- Step 1: Pour out enough Doritos to cover a cookie sheet.
- Step 2: Cover the Doritos with Buddig brand thinly sliced deli meats—torn lovingly into small pieces.
- Step 3: Add a generous coating of processed shredded cheddar cheese.

- Step 4: Bake in the oven at 350 degrees until the oil from the processed cheese is dripping onto the cookie sheet, or until you smell them burning…whichever comes first.
- Step 5: Enjoy!

Our family continues to share this delicacy each year. What began as a quick, inexpensive meal for a poor, young married couple became a treasured Christmas Eve tradition.

Next, the sleeping arrangements on Christmas Eve. We have four children—two boys and two girls. Normally, the boys slept in one room and the girls in another. But on Christmas Eve, mattresses were moved so that all four slept in one room. They would talk excitedly until, one by one, they were all asleep.

They were equipped with one walkie-talkie; I had another. When all four kids were awake on Christmas morning (usually, sometime between 4:00–5:00 a.m.), they would call me on the walkie-talkie. I would tell them to hold tight while I went out to the family room and started a fire in the fireplace, and Carol got the camera ready.

The time they were asked to spend waiting was not a time of impatience but rather a time of joyful anticipation.

When the wait was over, we would open their bedroom door, and Carol would snap a picture of them before they all ran out to the family room.

I know you are all thinking how adorable this is as you picture four little children doing this. However, you should know that this tradition continued well into their teens. As a matter of fact, when our oldest came home from college her freshmen year, she was the first to *ever* ask, "Are we still going to do this?"

There are so many other Christmas traditions we've enjoyed—decorating the tree, making presents for Mom, driving around to look at Christmas lights in their PJs…and talking about Jesus and His birthday. We also prayed together before we opened presents, went to Mass together, bought gifts for those less fortunate, and made it a point to say aloud how much we loved and appreciated one another.

For us, the weeks leading up to Christmas were full of expectant waiting—the excited feeling that something special was about to happen—and it always did.

To this day, it is the *traditions* our kids remember and cherish—not the memory of presents they received. Now that our children have their own families, they have begun their own traditions because they have recognized the value such traditions add to the season.

What prompted this walk down memory lane was something I read regarding the season of Advent. It said, "If you're sick of Christmas by December 25th, you haven't done Advent correctly."

Advent is a time of expectant waiting—the excited feeling that something special is about to happen.

Advent often gets lumped in with Lent. There are some similarities, but they are *not* the same. To illustrate the primary difference between Advent and Lent, we might use the analogy of housecleaning: Lent is spring cleaning; we purge and everything is scrubbed. Advent is getting your home ready for a special guest; we prepare our hearts for the coming of Jesus.

Lent is a season of repentance. Advent is a season of joyful preparation—serving as proof that there can be joy in waiting. It is a season of hopeful anticipation. As we heard in Luke's gospel, it is a time when "the winding roads shall be made straight, and the rough ways made smooth."

Advent is not only a liturgical season but also an annual faith tradition. There is value in acknowledging and carrying on traditions. We use symbols such as the Advent wreath to keep our focus on what is to come. The word *Advent* means "drawing near." As the birth of Jesus draws nearer, another candle is lit, with each candle dispelling the darkness a little more. Thus, the Advent wreath helps us to spiritually contemplate the great unfolding of salvation history, the infusion of light into a dark world.

There are Advent calendars that call us to daily action or reflection. Each day suggests something we can pray about or do that takes us outside of ourselves.

Here at St. Pius, we have the tradition of the *Christ in Christmas* tree, by which we are asked to share our gifts with the St. Philip Neri community.

These Advent traditions are all focused outward—away from self and toward God and others. Honoring the traditions shows what we value as a faith community and offers us a sense of belonging; we are a part of something bigger than ourselves. Traditions offer an excellent context for meaningful pause and reflection.

During this time of Advent reflection, the words we heard earlier from St. Paul's letter to the Philippians serve as encouragement. He wrote, "This is my prayer: that your love may increase ever more and more in knowledge and every kind of perception," to discern what is of value, "so that you may be pure and blameless for the day of Christ." Again, preparing our hearts for the coming of Jesus.

Traditions are not just old-fashioned things we repeat out of laziness or habit; they help us discern what is of value. By honoring traditions, we are not simply going through the motions. We are not saying, "We don't want to grow" or "We don't want to change." Rather, we are saying, "We want to remember."

For the secular world, the time leading up to Christmas is focused on Black Friday, Cyber Monday, crowded malls, and long checkout lines. By the time December 25 rolls around, they are exhausted. They just want to pack away Christmas and be done with it.

For Christians honoring the Advent season, the time leading up to Christmas is a time of joyful preparation and hopeful anticipation.

"If you're sick of Christmas by December 25th, you haven't done Advent correctly."

December 2018

Simon Did It

Fifth Sunday in Ordinary Time   Isaiah 6:1–8
                                1 Corinthians 15:1–11
                                Luke 5:1–11

I came to a decision last night that I wanted to share with you. Earlier this week, I read a news story about Deacon Lawrence Girard, a deacon serving in Dearborn Heights, Michigan. Deacon Lawrence is one hundred years old and is still assisting at eight Masses per week. Someone sent me that article and asked if I will still be serving St. Pius when I am one hundred years old. I thought about it and made a decision.

Fr. Jim is approximately ten years my senior. So I have decided that I will serve St. Pius until I am one hundred years old *if* Fr. Jim agrees to remain as pastor until he is 110.

The ball is in his court now.

I was ordained a deacon in 2012. When Bishop Coyne laid his hands on my head, the visible sign of God's sacramental grace, and invoked the blessing of ordination, my life was changed forever.

I remember feeling like Isaiah must have felt in today's first reading: "Here I am, Lord. Send me!"

By ordination, deacons are given the special duty of reading the gospel, expressed by the bishop in these words: "Strengthened by sacramental grace you are dedicated to the People of God, in the service of the liturgy, of the gospel, and of works of charity."

You may have noticed before coming to the ambo to read the gospel, I go first to the celebrant of the Mass. He offers me a special blessing that I might "proclaim the gospel worthily and well."

It is an honor to read the gospel. I take this role seriously; I don't want the gospel to be merely words on a page. I want the readings to come to life. To do this, I need to climb inside of them; I need to be a part of them. So I ask myself, "What must it have been like to be there when this happened? How would I have felt? How would I have responded?"

Today's readings offered a great opportunity for me to put on the skin of Simon and insert myself into the story. We heard the story of Simon's call—a life-changing event for him.

Consider the sequence of events in today's gospel. It began with Jesus, a stranger at the time, climbing into Simon's boat. It ended two or three hours later with Simon's life turned completely upside down—the direction of his life changed forever.

My ordination took less than two hours, but I had over five years to discern and prepare for it. Unlike Simon, I was able to make a calculated, prayerful decision over a long period of time. His entire conversion process occurred in a matter of hours.

This was more than a career change for Simon. It was not simply a matter of saying, "I'm not going to fish anymore." The gospel says, and I quote, "They left *everything* and followed him." Simon left his business, his home, his family—*everything*—to follow a man he'd just met.

My ordination has required me to sacrifice a certain amount of my personal time in service to the Church. However, unlike Simon, I have maintained my livelihood, I live in the same home, and my family is intact. Simon sacrificed everything.

It was not a temporary life change for Simon either. He didn't step away only to return to his former life at a later date. Simon, who would become Peter, ultimately became the rock upon which the entire Church was built.

What was it that transpired in those few short hours that completely changed Simon's life?

The story does not tell us what Simon was feeling or exactly what it was that triggered his life-changing decision. Jesus was decisive and spoke with authority. His words were captivating. He was powerful yet soft-spoken. He challenged yet spoke of love.

There was something different, something special about Jesus. This was made clear by Simon's willingness to accommodate the odd requests Jesus made. Simon had returned from an unsuccessful night of fishing. He just wanted to wash his nets, go home, and get some sleep.

Yet when Jesus climbed into his boat and said, "Take me out a short distance from the shore," Simon did it.

Simon had dropped his nets into the water over and over again throughout the night, catching nothing. He was a professional fisherman who knew these waters; and yet when this stranger with no fishing experience said, "Lower your nets for a catch," Simon did it.

In his lifetime, no one ever caught so many fish that their nets might tear. Simon knew catching that many fish was supernatural. He knew he'd witnessed a miracle. He was in the presence of something much bigger than himself and was frightened by what it meant for him. Yet when Jesus said, "Do not be afraid; follow me," Simon did it.

This gospel passage is a tremendous story of conversion. It is a story of an unwavering response to a vocational call. It is a story of faith and trust. However, the gospels are not just stories. The word *gospel* means "the revelation of Christ *or* something regarded as true and to be believed."

The gospels are a road map for us to follow. They are a glimpse into what living a life for Christ truly means.

Your life is a gospel story. *You* are the main character. Right now, Jesus is in your boat with you.

He is giving you instructions. If you listen to Him, He will guide your boat and tell you where to drop your nets. However, He will also challenge you to do difficult work, work that you may not immediately understand, work that may take you out of your comfort zone. He recognizes fear could get the best of you. Just as He did with Simon, Jesus is locking eyes with you and saying, "Do not be afraid. Follow me."

When Jesus asked Simon to convert his heart, he did it. Will you?

It's *your* gospel story. How *you* respond determines how the story ends.

May I suggest using the same response we heard from Isaiah: "Here I am, Lord. Send me!"

February 2019

Welcome Home

Fourth Sunday of Lent   Joshua 5:9–12
                                 2 Corinthians 5:17–21
                                 Luke 15:1–32

The following is the story of Amy and Joe, a story of reconciliation:

Joe began. "Near my house, there's a sign that reads, 'Please do not drink and drive.' There's a smaller sign underneath that reads, 'In honor of Amy.' Amy was a young lady I killed in 1992 while driving drunk on the freeway."

After the accident, Joe fled the scene. He was later arrested for second-degree murder. In the days that followed, he was overcome by what he had done.

"But God put some people in my life who made me understand what reconciliation was all about," Joe explained.

Joe spent the next seven and a half years behind bars. On January 6, 1999, he was released and went home to his family and friends.

When the weekend arrived, he and his wife discussed whether or not to attend church on Sunday. They decided yes, and when they arrived, the people of the church were waiting to welcome Joe and his family with open arms.

The oak trees surrounding the church had yellow ribbons around them, and there was a big banner at the entrance that said, "Welcome home, Joe!"

Not long after Joe's release, his mentor called to say that Amy's brother, Derek, wanted to meet with him. For years, Joe had prayed that God would help him reconcile with Amy's family.

That first meeting with Derek was several hours long. Derek told Joe how much he loved Amy and that he previously thought Joe was a monster who should get the electric chair for what he had done.

Joe told Derek something he had long wanted to say: "I'm really sorry for what I've done, and I hope that someday you can forgive me."

Not long after that meeting, Joe's mentor called again to say that Rick, Amy's father, wanted to meet with him too.

In a long meeting, Rick told Joe about the two days a year that he visits Amy's grave: on her birthday and on the anniversary of her death.

During that meeting, something miraculous occurred.

"Amy's father forgave me before I even asked him to forgive me," Joe said.

Joe's prayers for reconciliation were being answered.

He also met with Amy's mom, who asked him to watch a three-hour video of Amy's life before their meeting.

"I really got to know Amy that night," Joe said, "and how precious she was and what a tragedy it was that I took her life."

His relationship with Amy's family continued to grow, and both Joe and Derek were asked to participate in a restorative-justice event in front of hundreds of people.

That night, Amy's father approached Joe, hugged him, and said, "I love you, Joe." Even now, years later, Rick's actions and words still affect Joe.

"I killed his daughter," he said with emotion, "and he was able to give me a hug and say, 'I love you.' That is a true testament to the miracle of reconciliation."

The readings we hear throughout the Lenten season focus on forgiveness and reconciliation. We are directed to seek forgiveness for our own sinful deeds of course but also to *offer* forgiveness to others.

For example, in recent weeks, we heard Jesus explain to Peter that we must forgive our brother "*not seven times but seventy-seven times.*" We also heard Jesus encourage his disciples to *be merciful, just as the Father is merciful.* And on this Fourth Sunday of Lent, Jesus offers the parable of the prodigal son, the ultimate tale of forgiveness.

The words *forgiveness* and *reconciliation* are often used interchangeably. Forgiveness frees the sinner of guilt and shame. Once freed from guilt and shame, then what? That is where reconciliation comes in. Reconciliation is an added step, essential to nurturing a relationship.

Perhaps we can think of it in this way. Think of the sinner as a car going in reverse. When forgiveness is given, the brakes are applied, and the car slides into neutral. Forgiveness has neutralized the sin. It's good that the sinner is not going backward anymore, but it's not going forward either. Reconciliation puts the car in drive and allows it to begin moving forward.

In the story of the prodigal son, the son sought forgiveness from his father. In doing so, he said to his father, "Father, I have sinned against you. I no longer deserve to be called your son; treat me as you would treat one of your hired workers."

The father could have done just as the son suggested. He could have said, "I forgive you. I will now treat you as I would treat one of my hired workers." Had that occurred, the sins of the son would have been neutralized, but the relationship would not have moved forward. There would have been forgiveness without reconciliation.

Instead, the father *did* offer reconciliation. He immediately ordered his servants to bring his son "the finest robe and put a ring on his finger. Take the fattened calf and slaughter it. Then let us celebrate with a feast."

The parable of the Prodigal Son is not a simple story of forgiveness; it is one of forgiveness *and* profound, unconditional reconciliation.

Think about what prompted Jesus to tell the story; the Pharisees were bothered that Jesus was welcoming and eating with sinners.

What if it were a different scenario? Let's say the Pharisees watched as sinners came to Jesus and listed all the sinful things they had done. Then Jesus shook his finger at them, told them to stop their evil ways, and sent them away. Had that been the case, the

Pharisees would have approved, and the parable of the prodigal son would never have been told.

The Pharisees were not complaining because Jesus offered forgiveness; they were complaining because Jesus offered reconciliation. He offered the sinners the opportunity to return to the fold, to be welcomed, and to eat with him—to slip the car into "Drive" and move forward.

The Pharisees believed in conditional forgiveness; Jesus offered *un*conditional love.

In our second reading, Paul called upon the Corinthians to love as Jesus did. Paul told the Corinthians—and tells us today—that we are called to the *ministry of reconciliation*. When we answer that call, we become, as Paul described it, *ambassadors for Christ*.

As ambassadors for Christ, we speak and act on his behalf, offering both forgiveness and reconciliation.

We are ambassadors for Christ when we welcome home an estranged family member, no questions asked, or when we lovingly invite those who have left the Church to return. We are ambassadors for Christ when we spend time with and offer reassurance to anyone on the fringe who is seeking forgiveness and needs to feel valued.

Forgiveness is a beautiful gift. However, it was the *reconciliation* offered by Amy's family that allowed Joe to move forward. It was *reconciliation* that led the father of the prodigal son to say, "My son was dead and has come to life again; he was lost and has been found."

March 2019

Create Your Own Tipping Point

Third Sunday of Easter   Acts 5:27–32, 40–41
                                Revelation 5:11–14
                                John 21:1–19

    I have mentioned my former neighbor, Shirley, in past homilies. In those homilies, I alluded to the fact that Shirley could be a demanding, difficult woman. I assisted her for over nine years—cutting her grass, raking her leaves, shoveling her driveway, getting her mail, and whatever else was needed. Carol and I continued to care for her as she grew older and her health began to decline. Eventually, she was hospitalized and later moved to a nursing home. As a side note, Shirley is doing well and remains as cranky as ever.

    When she moved into the nursing home, she asked if I would sell all her belongings and oversee the sale of her house. She only trusted two people in the world, she said—me and her son. Her son Al, whom I had never met, was wheelchair-bound and was not able to help me with this task.

    This was not a simple request to sell a couple of chairs and a couch. Shirley's house was full—every room, the garage, the attic, and the outside shed—from floor to ceiling. Knowing this, I still did as she asked.

    After several months of work, the house was empty and ready to be sold.

    Although not very deacon-like, I did a happy dance on the day the sale on her house closed. No more extra grass-cutting, leaf-raking, or snow-shoveling. No daily checking in on Shirley or responding to her demands. It was the best of both worlds—Shirley was being well cared for, *and* I was not the one doing it. I was free; I no longer worked for Shirley.

God showed his sense of humor just two days later when I received a text from Shirley's son, Al. It read simply, "You need to take me over to see my mom." Not "Would you mind?" or "Is it possible?" It was just a statement of fact as to what my next duty was.

I took him to see his mom. On that day, nearly two years ago, I discovered I now work for Al. Depending on what's going on in his life, I receive anywhere from five to twenty-five texts a week from Al. They say things like "You can pick up my prescriptions today" or "I have a check that needs deposited." The closest I get to having a choice in the matter is when the text says, "Would you prefer to pick up my ClickList at Kroger at six or seven o'clock this evening?"

Recently, Al has had some health concerns of his own. He was hospitalized for a time and then transferred to a rehab facility. This past Tuesday, I received a text from him telling me I needed to bring him some clothes and other items from his apartment; and I, of course, did as he ordered. When I arrived at his room at the rehab facility, he did not seem his cranky self but looked and acted sad. We visited briefly. Before leaving, I surprised Al by asking if he wanted me to pray with him, something I had not done in the past.

He surprised *me* by saying, "Yes." I took his hands in mine, and we prayed. Tears welled up in his eyes. As I left, I heard him say softly, "Thank you."

On Thursday, I picked him up to take him to a doctor's appointment. While in my car, he asked if he could talk to me about something personal and began to cry. He said our prayer together made him realize something was missing; he needed Jesus in his life and wanted my help.

Like in today's gospel, Jesus was asking Al, "Do you love me?"

It was powerful. Al had reached a tipping point. Perhaps it was a response to his health concerns and the recognition of his own mortality, or maybe the prayer we shared ignited memories of a past relationship with God. Whatever it was, things became clearer for Al that day. He realized he needed to redirect his life and invite Christ to be a part of it.

We made plans to meet again soon to read some scripture together.

St. Peter was an impulsive, passionate, and energetic man who often acted without thinking. Sometimes, this worked out for him; many times, it did not.

Consider our experience of Peter throughout scripture and the number of times Jesus had to calm him down and explain things:

At the transfiguration, Peter got excited and suggested they immediately build three tents—one for Jesus, one for Moses, and one for Elijah. Jesus explained why he *shouldn't* do that.

At the Last Supper, Peter stopped Jesus in the midst of his lesson on servitude, telling him, "You will *not* wash my feet!" Jesus explained why he *must* wash his feet.

So Peter jumped impulsively in the opposite direction, telling Jesus, "Then wash my head and my hands too!" Jesus calmly explained why he *wouldn't* need to do that.

It was Peter who pulled out a sword and cut off the soldier's ear when Jesus was being arrested. Jesus explained there was *no* need for that.

In today's gospel, we heard, "When Simon Peter heard that it was the Lord, he tucked in his garment and jumped into the sea."

That's our impulsive Peter!

Moments later, Peter had an intimate encounter with Jesus—just the two of them face-to-face on the beach. It proved to be the tipping point for Peter. It was there that Jesus asked him three times, "Do you love me?" The gospel tells us that when Jesus asked the exact same question three times, *Peter was distressed*.

He likely wondered, "Is this Jesus's way of telling me he doesn't trust me?"

More likely, this was Jesus's way of saying, "Think this through, Peter. Reflect on the question, and carefully consider what I'm asking."

What happened on that beach changed the course of Peter's life; he no longer needed things explained to him. Soon thereafter, Jesus ascended to heaven and Peter was left in charge.

His goal was simple: Preach the gospel no matter what. It was a thoughtful, reflective answer to Jesus's question, "Do you love me?" He redirected his passion and energy toward an unwavering "Yes!"

In our reading from the Acts of the Apostles, we heard the high priest say to Peter, "We gave you strict orders, did we not, to stop teaching in that name? Yet you have filled Jerusalem with your teaching."

Peter said in reply, "We must obey God rather than men."

Basically, Peter said, "We can't stop, and we won't stop." He was all in.

Where are we on our faith journey? Is it time to redirect our efforts?

Are we sitting at one extreme or the other? Lost and feeling disconnected like Al? On fire for our faith but in need of focus and direction like Peter? Perhaps we are somewhere in between.

We *could* wait for circumstances or external forces to eventually lead us to a tipping point.

Or we can *choose* to redirect our life toward Christ. It is in our control.

Jesus is asking us right now, "Do you love me?"

How will we respond?

May 2019

Lawnmowers, Pickup Trucks, and Loving Others

Fifth Sunday of Easter

Acts 14:21–27
Revelation 21:1–5
John 13:31–35

I have some exciting news to share. I bought a new lawnmower last Saturday. This news is exciting on multiple levels. First, it's exciting because I'm a guy, and a lawnmower is a piece of power equipment. Second, I have needed a new lawnmower ever since the self-propelled mechanism died three years ago.

My excitement manifested itself in several ways. For instance, I took pictures of it and sent it to my sons and sons-in-law—who were quite impressed. I also timed how long it took me to cut the grass and shared the comparison between my *old* lawnmower time and my *new* lawnmower time with Carol. She was very supportive and pretended to be excited about it too. And I cut the grass twice this week—once because it needed cut, the second time just because I wanted to.

I experienced this same type of excitement last year when I gave my Toyota Camry away. It had 270,000 miles on it. I bought a new used pickup truck with only 80,000 miles—very exciting.

These examples of excitement come from the newness of the experience—a comparison of how I felt previously to how I feel now. My level of excitement is based upon personal experience. It's not about the brand of the lawnmower or the make and model of the truck. It's about the rush that comes with a new experience. It's about getting a fresh start, replacing something that was worn out or no longer working with something new or different or better.

Today's readings each speak to the new message Jesus brought to the world. Jesus made it clear that the old way was not working, and a new path was needed.

For many, it created excitement. We heard in the first reading that as Paul and Barnabas spread the good news to the Gentiles, they "made a considerable number of new disciples." The Gentiles had always been on the outside looking in, and Jewish law *kept* them as outsiders. Now here were Paul and Barnabas *inviting* them to follow the teachings of Jesus Christ to be a part of something new. The good news gave the Gentiles *hope*.

In today's second reading from Revelation, we heard: "I, John, saw a new heaven and a new earth. The former heaven and the former earth had passed away. The One who sat on the throne said, 'Behold, I make all things new.'"

There again is our word of the day—*new*. The message of *hope* found in the Book of Revelation is possible because Jesus Christ offered something new—"a new heaven and a new earth"—a new *vision* of heaven and a new *plan* for our life on earth.

What is that plan? It is simple, and we heard it directly from Jesus in today's Gospel: "I give you a new commandment: love one another as I have loved you."

The excitement of a new lawnmower came from my *hope* of an easier, quicker, and more efficient way to cut my lawn.

Jesus's message offered hope to his disciples. They, in turn, spread the good news; and it brought hope and excitement to the Gentiles. It can do the same for us today—the new commandment gives us hope for a better, more fulfilling life.

Those who have left the Church will use my own words against me. They will say, "I have no hope in the Church because nothing *is* new. It's the same Mass. It's the same message. Everything is always the same, and I don't get anything out of it."

Those who use that argument don't understand the new commandment of which Jesus spoke. If we love one another as Jesus loves us, we would not be focused solely on whether or not we "get anything out of it." We would *also* be looking for ways to put something *into* it.

I participate in many Masses; they are *not* all the same. The order of the Mass is the same, as are some of the common prayers. However, each Mass is unique. The priest celebrant, cyclical readings, the homily, and alternating Eucharistic prayers bring new elements to each Mass.

Even the actions that *are* repeated at every Mass offer a new opportunity to experience Christ in a very real way. Every time we see the priest elevate the host and the chalice and hear the words of consecration—"This is my body, this is my blood"—it should give us chills. It is a new opportunity to experience the unconditional love and sacrifice of Jesus firsthand.

Every time we receive Holy Communion, the minister says, "The Body of Christ," and we respond, "Amen." Same action, same words, but each time, it is a new opportunity to commit to our belief in Jesus. If our "amen" is mechanical and without feeling or conviction, then it truly is just more of the same. However, if our "amen" is said with conviction from the heart—if that "amen" means "Yes, I believe! I would stake my life on it!"—as it should, then we will have a new experience that brings us hope.

Each time we offer the sign of peace, something we do at every Mass, we have a new opportunity to experience community, to engage with the Body of Christ.

Mass is the fingerprint of Christ, and no two fingerprints are alike.

My new lawnmower does not change the fact that I am still cutting the grass. My new used pickup truck does not change the fact that I am still driving from point A to point B.

However, when we embrace new opportunities, we gain a new perspective.

If you get a new lawnmower every year, the one you buy this year may not excite you or bring you much joy. Likewise, if you believe your current life is fine just the way it is, the Mass or Jesus's new commandment to love one another may seem like old news—the same old news viewed through the same distorted lens.

The new commandment to love one another was expressed by Jesus nearly two thousand years ago. However, if we embrace that commandment with renewed conviction each day, we will experience life anew. We will usher in a new day filled with excitement and hope.

"Behold, I make all things new."

May 2019

Don't Be a Bystander

The Ascension of the Lord   Acts 1:1–11
                              Ephesians 1:17–23
                              Luke 24:46–53

When I was a classroom teacher, one of the subjects I taught was Psychology. For one lesson on perception, I conducted an experiment. Before I share the story of the experiment with you, please keep in mind it was 1987, and school safety and security concerns were much different than they are today.

I asked a friend of mine to enter my classroom as I was teaching. He was instructed to knock whatever I had in my hands to the floor, rummage through a couple of drawers, push books and papers off my desk, all while mumbling incoherently throughout. He then walked to the back of the room, looked out the window, returned to the front of the room, and exited.

The purpose of the experiment was to record the students' perception of the event, how much detail they could recall, and what variables affected their perception and recall. However, I discovered something else.

I told the students the police would be notified and would need as much information as possible. I said *if they were comfortable doing it*, I wanted them to put their name on a piece of paper and write down as many specific details as they could recall.

Of the thirty students in the class, only about half turned in a paper to me. Of those that did turn in a paper, several simply wrote that everything had happened too quickly or gave some other excuse to explain why they could not provide *any* details.

There were thirty witnesses to the event, but only twelve felt comfortable sharing what they experienced.

I am sure you have heard of instances of crimes, sometimes horrific crimes, taking place in front of a handful or even dozens of witnesses, and yet no one calls the police to make a report. Eyewitnesses took it all in, were appalled by what they saw, and yet did nothing. Those who were eventually identified as witnesses said they did not report the incident out of fear—fear of getting involved, fear of repercussions, fear of the unknown.

On the other end of the spectrum, each day, we are witnesses to the presence of Christ in our lives. We experience beauty in nature—a beautiful sunrise, a soft breeze blowing, flowers blooming. We feel warmth in our heart as we pray. We see the face of Christ in others. We are witnesses to all these things. We take it all in, are amazed by what we experience, and yet do nothing. What is our excuse for not sharing these experiences with others? What are we afraid of?

As we celebrate the Ascension of the Lord, our readings focus on the call to be witnesses. Before ascending, Jesus told his disciples, "It is written that the Christ would suffer and rise from the dead for the forgiveness of sins. You are *witnesses* of these things…you will be my witnesses to the ends of the earth."

In order to understand what it is that we, as today's disciples, are being called to, let's use this as our working definition of witness: "A witness is someone who has personal knowledge of something and can attest to that knowledge."

Jesus would take this definition a step further. Rather than "can attest to that knowledge," Jesus would say, "*must* attest to that knowledge." A witness to the faith is someone who has personal knowledge of Jesus Christ and must attest to that knowledge.

If we have the knowledge and *don't* attest to it, we are merely bystanders. That's why the two men dressed in white garments said to the disciples, "Men of Galilee, why are you standing there looking at the sky?" That was their way of encouraging the disciples *not* to be bystanders but rather to share the good news.

In accepting the role of bystander, we are allowing fear to dictate our actions.

Some level of fear is understandable. Expressing our faith leaves us vulnerable. How will people respond to us? How will we be viewed? Are we courageous enough to share our faith with others and acknowledge the role of Christ in our lives?

Jesus anticipated that the disciples would be afraid. That is why, in these weeks leading up to Pentecost, Jesus told the disciples repeatedly that they would not be alone in this effort. They would receive the gift of the Holy Spirit. This promise is repeated in all three of the readings today:

> In a few days you will be baptized with the Holy Spirit. (Acts 1:5)

> God will give you a Spirit of wisdom and revelation resulting in knowledge of him. (Ephesians 1:17)

> I am sending the promise of my Father upon you and you will be clothed with power from on high. (Luke 24:49)

It is clear when we speak and act on behalf of Christ, we do not speak and act alone. By virtue of our baptism, we have received the gift of the Holy Spirit.

Trying to wrap my mind around the concept of the Trinity gives me a headache, but I hold onto this simple image: God the Father is our creator, God the Son is our example, and God the Holy Spirit is our voice.

This understanding of the Holy Spirit certainly ties in with our role as witnesses to the faith. Using our voice is what distinguishes witnesses from bystanders. However, for many of us, using our voice scares us the most.

It is important to understand that using our voice does not have to mean preaching from the pulpit or speaking into a megaphone on a crowded street corner. When Jesus instructed his disciples to be witnesses to what they had seen, he was not sending them off to give prepared speeches to the world.

Using our voices may indeed refer to *talking* about our faith. It *might* include preaching from the pulpit or speaking into a megaphone. However, it can also be casual conversations between friends, sharing God moments you've experienced in your day. It can be leading a prayer before you begin a staff meeting or before you sit down to a business lunch. It can be offering to pray with someone who has just shared a difficult situation she is facing in her life. It can be a personal, one-on-one discussion with someone whose beliefs are different than our own.

However, when it comes to being witnesses to our faith, we can also use our voice in other ways.

When we share our faith on social media, we are using our faith voice. When we read faith-based books, articles, or posts and then share them with others, we are using our faith voice. When we live life joyfully and show love and compassion for others, we are using our faith voice. When we stand up for the rights of those most vulnerable, we are using our faith voice.

To have a strong faith and not share it is selfish. By refusing to be a witness, we become a mere bystander. Don't be a bystander. Don't just stand there looking at the sky.

June 2019

Sure and Certain Hope

Nineteenth Sunday in Ordinary Time
Wisdom 18:6–9
Hebrews 11:1–2, 8–12
Luke 12:35–40

Many of you know that my wife, Carol, has retired after working nearly twenty-five years at St. Pius X School and Bishop Chatard. On that topic, before I begin my homily, I'd like to answer some of the pressing questions I have been asked lately.

With a great deal of concern, people have asked, "How is Carol doing? Is she okay? Is she adjusting to retirement? Any regrets about retiring?"

Let me say this as clearly and emphatically as I can: I assure you, Carol is *fine*. Please do not spend another minute worrying about Carol and her adjustment to retirement. She has never once looked back. She sleeps well at night and does whatever she wants during the day. So yes, I think she's "adjusting."

As a matter of fact, in the history of retirement, I would dare say *no one* has adjusted more quickly and efficiently than my wife.

Please put your concerns about Carol aside. She is just fine.

Please allow me to process aloud in my homily this morning.

Several words have been bouncing around in my head of late: the phrase *sure and certain* and the words *faith* and *hope*.

I have had two profound experiences of death recently.

Two weeks ago, I was honored to be at a parishioner's bedside when he died, losing his battle with cancer. I was able to pray a decade of the Rosary with the family just moments before he passed away. There was an immediate emotional response to the death, of course—crying, sadness. It was quickly replaced, however, with the sharing of beautiful memories, stories of Brian as a beloved husband, father, and sibling. I heard joy in the voices of family members as they spoke with unwavering faith and confidence about their loved one entering heaven. They expressed no doubt; they were sure and certain of this outcome.

In a homily I delivered back in early May, I mentioned Al. I described him as the wheelchair-bound, rough-around-the-edges son of my former next-door neighbor, Shirley. I cared for Shirley as she became physically unable to do many things around her home, eventually moving to a nursing home for full-time care. I shared with you how her son Al had taken up where Shirley left off. He expected me, in no uncertain terms, to take him to appointments, pick up his prescriptions, and bring him his groceries as directed.

I also shared that there had been a breakthrough with Al. He was softening. He decided he wanted Jesus in his life and asked my help in making that happen. We decided we would study scripture together. He didn't have a Bible, so I brought mine when we met.

This past Wednesday, Al died of a heart attack while making himself dinner. As we heard in today's gospel, "You must be prepared, for at an hour you do not expect, the Son of Man will come."

I had the difficult task of breaking the news to his mom, eighty-six-year-old Shirley, at the nursing home. Much like the previously mentioned death, there was the initial crying and sadness. Then Shirley began sharing stories of Al. Stories of Al growing up, the two of them running a business together, how tight the bond between them had always been. After spending time with her, I was preparing to leave when she said, "I hope Al is in heaven."

I responded, "My hope is in the resurrection, and that was Al's hope too." I added, "I think he made it."

You would have to know Shirley to really appreciate this, but she said, "I'm gonna say some extra prayers just in case."

For me, the first sentence in today's reading from the letter to the Hebrews helped shed light on these two recent deaths.

We heard this: "Faith is the realization of what is hoped for and evidence of things not seen. *Again:* Faith is the realization of what is hoped for and evidence of things not seen." I was captivated by this sentence when I read it for the first time. I read it over and over again and found such beauty in it but was unsure why.

I almost didn't include it in my homily because it was so challenging to wrap my mind around. My brain was suddenly flooded with questions. Are faith and hope even compatible? If I have faith, true faith, is hope necessary? Doesn't hope imply at least *some* level of doubt? Should someone of strong faith have *hope* in the resurrection? That's what I told Shirley—I used those exact words: "My *hope* is in the resurrection." Shouldn't my faith make our resurrection sure and certain?

There are those words: *sure and certain, faith, hope*.

To muddy the waters even further, these are the words the celebrant says at the end of a funeral Mass. It is the prayer of commendation: "Into your hands, Father of mercies, we commend our brother, in the *sure and certain hope*, that together with all who have died in Christ, he will rise with Him on the last day."

There it is again: "in the sure and certain hope" of the resurrection. Is using *sure and certain* alongside "hope" appropriate?

I decided to turn to someone *much* older and somewhat wiser, so I contacted Fr. Jim. I was sure and certain that if our pastor didn't know the answer, he would make something up for me.

His response was actually quite insightful and helped clear my muddled thoughts.

These were his words: "Think of it this way. I'm not sure and certain of the resurrection. It is my *hope* that is sure and certain. A practical example: I have a sure and certain hope of getting a job because the interview went so well. I am not sure and certain that I will get the job, but my *hope* is sure and certain based on my experience with the interview.

Sometimes we speak of having a faint hope. This signifies that we might be overwhelmed by doubt or lack of faith—the *hope* is not strong.

To say "sure and certain hope" indicates our hope is very strong. It is so strong that it has helped me overcome my doubts."

And here is my favorite line from his response: "A sure and certain hope crushes any temptation to despair."

Back to Hebrews: "Faith is the realization of what is hoped for and evidence of things not seen." Faith allows us to consider the evidence that our life experiences offer. I am not scientifically able to prove that I have seen, touched, or heard God. However, I have the sure and certain hope that when I saw the sunrise this morning, it was God's handiwork. I have the sure and certain hope that when I held Shirley's hand, God was holding mine. I have the sure and certain hope that when I heard Brian's last breath, it was God whispering that the resurrection is real.

The fruits of faith are realized when what we hope for is attained.

As for Al, I remember the tears in his eyes when he told me he wanted a relationship with Jesus. I heard Shirley tell me that Al was a good son and a good man. On Friday, two days after his death, I walked through his apartment. Sitting on the arm of his favorite chair was a brand-new Bible he had apparently ordered online. I know in my heart he intended to use it.

I have a sure and certain hope in his resurrection.

August 2019

Who's on First?

Twenty-fifth Sunday in Ordinary Time   Amos 8:4–7
1 Timothy 2:1–8
Luke 16:10–13

There have been hundreds, perhaps thousands of volumes of work written on the topic of Christian morality—lengthy dissertations that enlighten us on the causes and types of sin and encourage us to stay on the straight and narrow path in order to maintain a "right relationship" with God. Scholars study for years and spend thousands of dollars to acquire graduate degrees with a focus on this topic.

Today, I am going to save you years of time and thousands of dollars. I am going to share the basic tenets of Christian morality with you in the course of one homily. (You're welcome.)

I will offer a philosophical viewpoint that examines the big picture, a theoretical viewpoint that explores the problem, and a practical viewpoint that offers a solution.

On the philosophical side, well-known Christian writer, C. S. Lewis, said this: "You can't get second things by putting them first; you can only get second things by putting first things first. Put first things first and we get second things thrown in. Put second things first and we lose both first and second things."

Let me repeat that: "You can't get second things by putting them first; you can only get second things by putting first things first. Put first things first and we get second things thrown in. Put second things first and we lose both first and second things."

Lewis's point? Putting God first is the only path to true Christian discipleship. It's about setting firm priorities, not constantly grasping at the newest or next best thing. It's about staying focused on what's most important.

I'm no C. S. Lewis, but on the theoretical side, the *struggle* of Christian morality can be thought of in these simple terms: Human beings desire a right relationship with God, but sometimes, often in the heat of the moment, we desire something else more.

Most of our destructive or sinful behavior is carried out with full knowledge and deliberate consent. In other words, we know it's wrong but choose to do it anyway. In that moment, we desire the adrenaline rush or the self-gratifying results of the behavior more than our desire for a right relationship with God.

Echoing Lewis's thinking, our priorities are out of whack. Every such behavior takes us further down the wrong path. We are our own worst enemy; we are the primary obstacle on our personal path to true Christian discipleship.

Finally, on the practical side, today's gospel passage from Luke states things very clearly: We can't serve two masters. Often, while on our lifelong journey toward God, we come to a fork in the road. We allow shiny objects to take us off course. We are drawn to different gods.

Luke wrote, "No servant can serve two masters. You cannot serve both God and mammon."

We may have heard *mammon* described as possessions or material wealth. However, for our purposes it is defined as "*all* worldly things that compete for our attention, our desire and our dedication."

This *may* include possessions or material wealth—a large home, a nice car, or a full bank account. However, it could also be a relentless pursuit of success or power. It could be addictive behaviors—drugs, alcohol, pornography, or gambling. It might even be something as seemingly innocuous as spending three nights a week out with the boys. It can be weekend athletic schedules that prevent us from attending Mass.

With the exception of a few I mentioned, these things are not intrinsically bad or evil. However, when they become our priority—

when there is a distorted desire or love of these things—it can cause us to drift further away from God. We are serving the wrong master. Or as C. S. Lewis would say, "The second thing has become the first thing."

In today's second reading, we heard a passage from Paul's First Letter to Timothy.

In the passage, Paul encouraged his friend and protégé, Timothy, to keep his priorities in line. Timothy had been put in charge of the large and growing church in Ephesus. He was young to have a position of such honor and power. He could easily have fallen prey to misplaced priorities and been enamored by the perks of his new position.

Paul cautioned Timothy when he wrote: "There is one God. There is also one mediator between God and men, the man Christ Jesus, who gave himself as ransom for all."

Paul learned from his own life experience that we are imperfect beings: We sin; we stumble and fall. Our actions take us out of balance when it comes to our relationship with God. We struggle when trying to get back in balance on our own. Jesus Christ, Paul wrote, acts as our mediator, our go-between.

The path to God the Father goes through Jesus. Who better to mediate the relationship between human beings and God than Jesus—fully human and fully divine?

Christian morality in a nutshell: The moral Christian aligns his priorities with the will of God and acts accordingly, focusing on what's most important. Our primary desire must be for Him.

Some of us may walk away from today's gospel disappointed, asking ourselves why it appears to be an either-or situation. I can have God, or I can have my stuff; I can't have both. I would say you can *have* both, you just can't *serve* both.

In a later chapter of Luke, Jesus will tell a rich young man that following the commandments is not enough. In order to attain eternal life, Jesus tells him to sell all his belongings, give the money to the poor, and *then* come and follow Him. We are told the man went away sad, for he had many possessions.

God is not presenting us with an either-or choice. He is challenging us to reflect upon the importance we place on worldly things. Are these things competing for our attention, our desire, and our dedication? Are our priorities out of whack?

Jesus was not challenging the rich young man because he had many possessions. He was challenging him because He knew these possessions had become gods. The man's world revolved around his stuff.

Jesus attempted to act as mediator, bringing him back into alignment with the will of God by redirecting his focus.

At morning prayer on Friday, I came upon these heartfelt words Tobit proclaimed to God: "Happy are those who love you…and happy those who rejoice in *your* prosperity."

We are not losing out when we place more importance on God. We are simply aiming for a different type of prosperity.

September 2019

About the Author

Deacon Rick Wagner has spent over thirty-five years working as a teacher, coach, and administrator in Catholic high schools. He has served as principal at two different Catholic high schools in the Indianapolis area.

Deacon Rick served as the director of the Permanent Deacon Formation program for Saint Meinrad Seminary and School of Theology for three years before returning to the high school scene and is currently serving as president of St. Theodore Guerin High School in Noblesville, Indiana.

He was ordained in 2012 and is assigned to St. Pius X Parish in Indianapolis.

He has published two additional books, *Remember What's Important* (2011) and *Fifty Homilies from the Deacon's Desk* (2016).

www.ingramcontent.com/pod-product-compliance
Lightning Source LLC
Chambersburg PA
CBHW031944161224
19091CB00042B/486